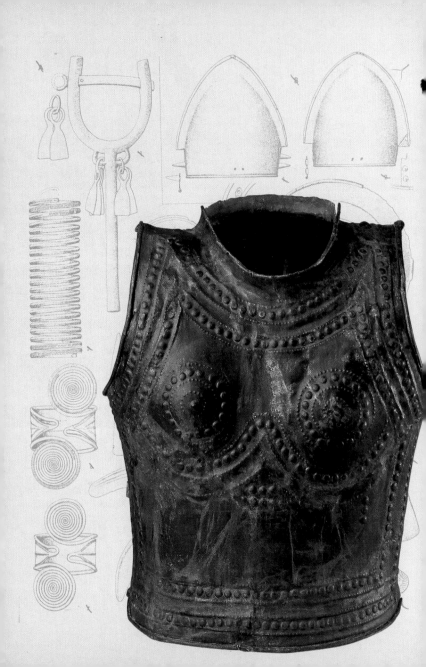

CONTENTS

THE BRONZE AGE IN EUROPE
GODS, HEROES AND TREASURES

Jean-Pierre Mohen and Christiane Eluère

The Bronze Age takes us back to the heroic legendary world of Homer, a glorious tradition that for a long time seemed devoid of any factual basis. After a century and a half of discoveries and analysis, however, the European Bronze Age we have come to understand impresses with its originality and the remarkably advanced societies it produced.

CHAPTER 1

DID THE BRONZE AGE EXIST?

Homer (opposite, "singing the *Iliad* at the gates of Athens") captured the imagination of many a reader. Heinrich Schliemann was the first to try to show that behind the legend there had in fact been a Trojan War in the Bronze Age, as can be seen in his excavation log (right), which he kept from February to June 1873.

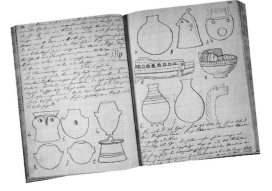

Themes drawn from the *Iliad* and the *Odyssey* have been taken up again from century to century. Thus, the siege of Troy, widely depicted in pottery of Classical antiquity, became a favorite theme of the Renaissance. Left: a painting by Daniel van Heil (c. 1604–62). Pieter Bruegel the Elder also painted a large fresco on the subject.

In narrating the Trojan War, Homer evoked an age that did not yet know iron, except as a precious metal, and relied on bronze to provide its arms, jewelry, tools, and cult objects. We have labeled it the Bronze Age and called its valiant warriors, like Achilles or Odysseus, heroes. The kings of the Bronze Age lived in palaces built inside fortified cities such as Mycenae, Pylos, and Troy. Their gods, Zeus, Athena, Poseidon, took part in daily life. Writing was not unknown to them. The Bronze Age, then, was the cradle of European history.

What was the Bronze Age?

The *Iliad* and the *Odyssey* are customarily considered a formalized account, made about 700 BC by the poet or poets known as Homer, of an ancient oral tradition that was believed to go back to the 2nd millennium BC. Ancient authors, writing in both Greek and Latin, considered the narrated acts to be true events. Was Homer a posthumous witness? The question has dogged every investigator of this period and is still asked today. Before any form of writing was recognized, and even later, with the deciphering of the tablets of Linear B, the *Iliad* was considered the earliest reference to Greek antiquity. The Homeric texts, read and studied by many generations of humanists, undoubtedly have contributed to creating a certain image of Greece. Their account of the Trojan War, in particular, fed the curiosity of the Romantic era in the 19th century, the first period

to take up the question of the Bronze Age's reality. And Homer's works held a dominant place in the education and research of Heinrich Schliemann, the man who discovered the site of Troy.

The development of archaeology and spectacular discoveries at the turn of the 20th century have renewed interest in ancient texts and inspired further study. These works offer opportunities for comparison and dating that have proved particularly valuable in the study of a protohistoric period. Epigraphists, historians, and archaeologists have pored over these writings, trying to separate fable from historic truth. With each new discovery, another clue contributes to the reinterpretation of these texts. Thus, the legend of Odysseus of the bronze spear, a fabulous epic that was recited long before Homer, continues to inspire questions and discoveries about a mythical period.

The theory of the three ages

Since the end of the 18th century, antiquarians and geologists had observed that ruins from the past could be classified by means of not simply the materials that

During Greco-Roman antiquity, the Homeric tradition was a source of inspiration not only for poets but also for visual artists. About 480 BC, on this red-figured cup by the potter Calliades, the artist Douris painted the combat of Ajax and Hector. The two heroes, supported by their tutelary gods—two Olympians who remain in the background—are fighting with hoplite arms of the 5th century BC. This "modernizing" of the warriors' appearance is typical of the epic tradition and does not essentially change the evidence of the heroic valor of Ajax and Hector. The earliest inscription of a text by Homer was engraved on a cup dated 725 BC, found in a tomb in Ischia, near Naples. It reads: "The cup of Nestor was most sweet to drink of. But whoever shall drink of this one, will be seized with desire for Aphrodite of the fair crown."

Many artists in the 19th century accompanied archaeologists in their efforts to reconstruct the life of a remote past. In 1897 Fernand Cormon drew this sketch titled *Bronze and Iron* to decorate the paleontology hall of the Museum of Natural History in Paris. Cormon strove for great precision in his reconstructions and contributed to the success of the new discipline of prehistory and its three ages. For this drawing he borrowed gestures and techniques observed in factories (the shapes of the crucible and forceps, the ovens in the background) and placed them in an archaic outdoor context with generalized habitations. In his sketch *Fishing*, drawn the same year (opposite), he mixed characters with realistic postures (the fisherman pulling the net) and academic poses (such as the woman and child). The late-19th-century vision of prehistory was an imaginary montage, of some interest because it attempted a reconstruction of prehistoric life though marred by anachronisms.

constitute them but also the techniques required for their construction. They found that this scheme made it possible to order them in time. The inspiration for this method came from the old model of the three ages of man, which the Roman poet and philosopher Lucretius had proposed in his treatise *On the Nature of Things,* written in the 1st century BC. Danish antiquarian Christian Jürgensen Thomsen (1788–1865) vindicated the method while classifying the collections of the

A very different approach from that of the artists of prehistory was taken by Christian Jürgensen Thomsen (below, in 1848), who classified man-made objects in the same way he would a natural history collection. Differences in materials—stone, bronze, and iron—determined the classification, which constituted the system of the three ages. It had the merit of being grounded in the archaeological collections, and it remains pertinent today, as current studies continue to base their analyses on observations of the objects themselves, which can be restored through archaeometric methods. Thus, Müller-Karpe in

National Museum of Denmark in Copenhagen. He in fact perceived an age of stone, the oldest, then of bronze, and finally iron. He insisted on the need to conduct not just typological but also technological comparisons and to study collections rather than individual objects. About 1850, one of his pupils, J. J. A. Worsaae (1821–85), a Swede, continued his work. From then on, archaeologists had an instrument at their disposal for situating their discoveries in time. To increase their understanding of a ruin, they did not hesitate to consult other specialists such as zoologists and geologists, thus practicing the interdisciplinary approach that would become the rule in archaeology. Worsaae confirmed the idea of a Bronze Age and distinguished two periods, characterized by funerary practices: first burial, then cremation.

The Swede Oscar Montelius (1843–1921) was the first to work out a typological approach to the Bronze Age. Inspired by evolutionist theories, in 1885 he defined one

1980 used the typology of archaeological ruins as a point of departure for reflections on the degree of historic reconstruction of societies in their socioeconomic context.

of his essential principles: every type of object evolves in response to a technical improvement or a change of style. Thus, the ax blade is at first flat, then flanged, then given a thick butt, then winged, and finally

socketed, which provided the best method for attaching a handle. In comparing the Nordic typologies with those of Italy, Montelius could establish traditions by means of categories of objects: axes, fibulae, bronze dishes. The study of burials then assumed special importance, because the offerings they contained are of necessity contemporary with the closing of the tomb. By typological cross-checking, Montelius set up a relative chronology of the European Bronze Age, which he attempted to relate to certain historic dates in Mesopotamia or Egypt, especially the date of the Exodus of the Jews from Egypt.

The Bronze Age and the origin of nations

The passionate interest of powerful men in Bronze Age excavations spurred public excitement and furthered research on the period. King Frederick VII of Denmark (1808–63) personally took part in excavations in tumuli. These mounds covered up oak tombs that had been particularly well preserved thanks to the humidity contained in the mass of the mound. The tannin of the oak had preserved the chitinous and organic matter, such as the hair and skin of the dead, as well as their woven wool clothing and the wooden and metal offerings. Frederick VII saw a connection between these remains and the mysterious drawings chipped into the rocks of southern Scandinavia depicting the same objects. For him, Bronze Age culture already expressed the identity of Scandinavian society.

Still in the 1860s, Napoléon III, an amateur historian and author of a monograph on Julius Caesar (1865), also researched the origin of the French nation, which he felt was reflected in the specific typologies of the Bronze Age. This viewpoint was disputed by the archaeologists

Oscar Montelius (left) in 1885 established a periodic chronology of the Nordic Bronze Age:
• Period 1 (1450–1250 BC): first appearances of copper from central Europe;
• Period 2 (1250–1050): abundant copper, burial in tumuli, under British influence, period of wooden coffins;
• Period 3 (1050–900): more numerous cremations, under pressure from central Europe;
• Periods 4 and 5 (900–550): Late Bronze Age and transition to the Iron Age.
This classification refined Thomsen's system of the three ages. It remains the point of departure for current research on the Nordic Bronze Age.

Frederick VII of Denmark was present in 1863 in Skodsborg at the excavation of a tumulus from the Bronze Age (engraving at left), which led to the revelation of coffins hollowed from the trunks of trees (below). The king presented Napoléon III with an archaeological collection inventoried in 1862 in the new National Museum of Antiquities at St.-Germain-en-Laye near Paris. The two monarchs' shared enthusiasm for archaeology reflects a similar interest in the origins of their nations,

of the Germanic Roman Central Museum of Mainz, especially Ludwig Lindensschmidt (1809–93), who all considered, for their part, that these typological nuances were meaningful only in relation to Germanic culture, the sole heir of a possible Bronze Age.

The abundance of discoveries led to the publication of the first monographs, such as those by Ernest Chantre (*Palethnologie de l'âge du bronze rhodanien* [Paleoethnology of the Rhône Bronze Age], Lyons, 1875) or Gabriel de Mortillet, whose *Musée préhistorique* (Prehistoric Museum, 1880) is a vast synthesis on the evolution of prehistoric and protohistoric cultures, for which he established a chronology.

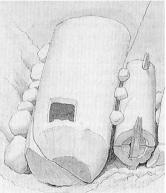

as well as curiosity about the individuals of the Bronze Age and their tumuli—the first monuments of original cultures.

The rediscovery of Bronze Age Greece

A brilliant businessman, son of a pastor in Mecklenburg, Germany, passionate about Homer, and converted somewhat late in life to archaeology, Heinrich

Schliemann (1822–90) wanted to bring the poet's world back to life. It was his ambition to identify the sites of the *Iliad* and the *Odyssey*. In 1870 he started the excavation of the hill of Hisarlik, in western Turkey, where he expected to rediscover the remains of the city of Troy. The spectacular discoveries he made there, especially the so-called Treasure of Priam, impressed specialists and seemed to demonstrate the authenticity of the Homeric site, even if, subsequently, these adornments and vessels of gold and silver proved far older than Schliemann had thought. Yet the excavations, continued by American archaeologist Carl Blegen, would later confirm the importance of the site and its probable identification with the mythic city of Troy, destroyed in the 14th or 13th century BC.

Meanwhile, beginning in 1874, Schliemann dug up the gold treasures of the princely tombs at Mycenae, thus revealing a civilization that had been memorialized by Homer's epics long after its material culture had totally disappeared. After Mycenae, other Homeric cities were excavated: Tiryns by Schliemann and Pylos by

With Schliemann, intuition inspired a tireless quest for antiquity among ancient landscapes and habitations. Arriving in Ithaca, he noted, "Each hill and each rock, each fountain and olive grove breathe Homer and the *Odyssey;* we are transported by a leap across a hundred generations." Below: Trojan excavations about 1873.

Blegen, who discovered numerous tablets at these sites (composed in a writing that came to be called Linear B) which when deciphered attested clearly to the city's identity.

Another discoverer of Aegean civilization, Sir Arthur Evans (1851–1941), received his training as an archaeologist at Oxford and Göttingen, Germany. Beginning in 1900 he undertook searches in Crete, particularly in the so-called Palace of Minos (the mythical king known from the legends of Theseus and the Minotaur) at Knossos, and for nearly forty years he struggled to restore its walls, sculpture, and frescoes.

A rthur Evans (below, at Knossos) brought to archaeology the problem of reconstructing remains and ruins. He had no qualms about relying on his imagination to communicate his vision (above, the throne room of the Palace of Minos).

Historical methods

The discovery, in less than fifty years, of evidence that extended Greek history back an additional ten centuries led archaeologists to ask some basic questions. Who had been responsible for an art of such precocity and originality in relation to later developments of Greek civilization? Had it been produced by an indigenous population or by peoples from the north?

One major theory proposed in the mid-20th century assumes that before the Bronze Age, the population of Greece—as well as of the entire Mediterranean basin—came from outside, probably from the north and east. Such migrations, according to Nancy Sandars (1978), were accompanied by the movement of "sea peoples" in Corsica, Egypt, and elsewhere.

This theory was also applied by the German archaeologists Wolfgang Kimmig and, later, Hermann Müller-Karpe to central and western Europe, to explain the phenomenon of what are called "urnfields," necropolises for cremation that appeared progressively in successive migrations from east to west. These invasions led to the arrival of the Achaeans, then the Dorians, in Greece. In the 1970s, English scholar Colin Renfrew, criticizing the "new archaeology," cast doubt on these grand syntheses, replacing them with a systems approach, which explains the cultural changes by internal evolution within societies.

Scientific methods

At this point, archaeologists turned to physicochemical methods to determine the characteristics of the remains being uncovered. For the study of ancient metals, Martin Heinrich Klaproth, the first professor of chemistry in Berlin in 1810,

Marcelin Berthelot (below, in his laboratory at the Collège de France) attempted to evaluate the chemical and alchemical knowledge of the ancients, both from written texts and by studying the composition of copper objects such as these arms (above) from Susa, Persia (Iran).

stands as a precursor. He introduced analytical methods, but his procedures had the disadvantage of being fairly destructive. In 1869 Ernst von Bibra made a synthesis of all this research, while in France Marcelin Berthelot devoted himself to Egyptian and Persian bronzes collected by Jacques de Morgan. Not until the use of spectroscopy in 1935 by the German J. Winckler was substantial progress made in the study of the composition of protohistoric metals. Around the 1960s, laboratories in Stuttgart, Oxford, London, St.-Germain-en-Laye, Paris, and Rennes, as well as Bochum in Germany, Moscow, and Philadelphia began to draw up treatises on the composition of these metals. R. F. Tylecote made a synthesis of these studies and defined the principles of a paleometallurgy.

With the development of geological investigations, the earth sciences were summoned to unlock the secrets of the metallic objects' surroundings. Knowledge of the materials' origins and the study of their means of transport, especially by sea, were aimed at evaluating systems of exchange and defining economic and possibly diplomatic horizons. A true paleoethnology of Bronze Age society has thus been sketched out since the 1960s, thanks to the methods of archaeometry, the application of analytical techniques from the physical sciences and engineering to archaeological materials.

Finally, the progress of dating methods—carbon 14, thermoluminescence, and dendrochronology—had a

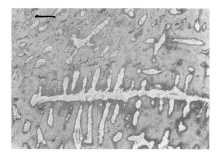

Paleometallurgy studies mine remains and ancient methods of production: reduction furnaces, production of ingots, casting of metal in molds. Metallographic and microscopic examination of a copper bead (left) found in southern France, in a 3rd-millennium BC archaeological context, reveals the conditions of the fusion of copper and of its slow cooling (below, the structure of copper grains, as it appears on a metallographic cross section studied under the microscope with a magnification of 200). The particle accelerator and X-ray fluorescence have been employed by the research laboratory of the French National Museums at the Louvre to determine the composition of metals and their impurities.

determining influence on the perception of several problems. These include the autonomy of metallurgical centers in eastern Europe in relation to those of Anatolia; the consequences of the eruption of Thera on the destruction of the Minoan palace period; the abrupt end of lakeside settlements in regions near the Alps; and the relations of Bronze Age Europe with the first Near Eastern and Egyptian empires.

Writing: a new element

Evidence of a first attempt at hieroglyphic writing dating to the 5th millennium is offered by clay tablets found at Tărtăria (Romania). These have a counterpart in the terra-cotta seal stones of Karanovo VI culture, presenting indecipherable signs. No further such examples were found.

Evans in Crete unearthed several forms of writing: hieroglyphs of the type found on the Phaistos disk, Linear A, and Linear B on tablets of raw clay, hardened by the flame of conflagrations. The first two nonalphabetic forms are attributed to the Minoans. The deciphering of Linear B in 1952 by Michael Ventris and John Chadwick revealed that it definitely related to a language that was common to the cities of Knossos, Mycenae, and Pylos, and that this language was already, around 1300 BC, a form of Greek.

These documents allow us to rethink the question of the origins of the Indo-European family of languages, to which most of the European languages belong, and to study more deeply the origins of the identity of each great European community. If the Greek language was spoken from the end of the Bronze Age, Celtic and Illyrian, for instance, were probably also introduced at the same period. Under these conditions, the formation of the large Indo-European linguistic units would be older than

The oldest form of writing known in Europe is engraved on tablets from Tărtăria (Romania), dated from the 5th millennium BC, which present a complex hieroglyphic system. They were discovered in the context of highly organized settlements that also had the oldest development of metallurgy and goldsmithing in Europe. This writing has not been deciphered.

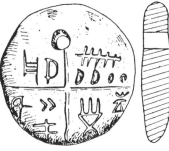

Tablets written in Linear B (left, example from Pylos, c. 1200) contain rough accounting drafts that could be retranscribed onto parchment. Now deciphered, they teach us about palace life. Linear A (below) remains a mystery, despite similarities with the later Linear B. The Phaistos

previously thought. This formation would be part of a complex process that groups together certain socioagricultural ways of life, a process that archaeology traces back to the beginning of the Neolithic Age rather than relating to exterior pressures exerted by invasions. Speculation about invasions has not advanced our understanding of the genesis of these multiple facets of the same large linguistic family. Other written sources also shed light on this period, such as the texts of the contemporary historic societies, Egypt and Mesopotamia. Thus, up to the end of the reign of Amenhotep III (1417–1379 BC), the Cretans and Mycenaeans were often mentioned in Egyptian texts; beginning in 1370 the Mycenaeans alone were cited and seem to have dominated the Cretans. This testimony is valuable for documenting one of the important changes that moved Europe toward history— into the heart of the Bronze Age.

disk (17th century BC), older than both, is entirely covered with hieroglyphics, possible imitations of Egyptian writing, which remain totally unreadable.

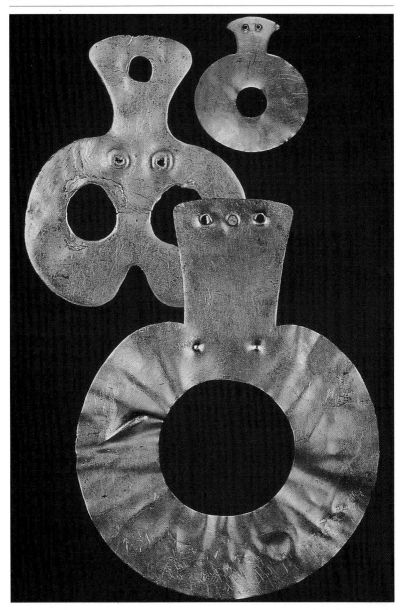

The earliest evidence of metallurgy in Europe, using copper and gold, has been found in Neolithic sites dating from just before 4000 BC. In the following period, called the Chalcolithic, experimentation with metalworking techniques between the 4th and 2nd millennia BC led to the creation of an alloy of copper and tin— bronze. It would bring profound changes to human society.

CHAPTER 2

THE FIRST USES OF METALS

These gold female idols (opposite) found recently in Greece are amulets of a type first seen in the 5th millennium BC. The largest is 6 inches, or 15 centimeters, high. Right: a copper ingot from Cyprus in the form of an oxhide, as seen in frescoes in Egypt, which imported them. Weighing about 22 pounds (10 kilograms), they could be carried on the shoulder.

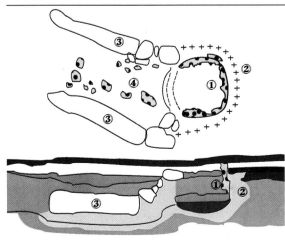

A reduction furnace in Timna, Israel (2nd millennium BC), consists of a small chamber with scarified, or scratched, walls (1) 20 inches (50 centimeters) long on each side, buried in a ditch (2) filled with charcoal. Here, the copper ore was reduced. In front of the furnace, a passageway lined with stones (3) allowed the metallurgist to work the bellows in the fireplace and, on completing the operation, to remove the mixture of slag and of copper nodules (4).

The emergence of metal was neither an isolated phenomenon nor a chance occurrence but rather a link in a socioeconomic evolution that involved long-distance trading, advanced knowledge of minerals and ores and their thermal reactions, as well as the presence of specialized artisans.

Emergence of the first metals in the Near East

The first metals to be worked were basically copper and gold, and the first alloys, of copper and arsenic, gave the period its name: Chalcolithic. The earliest attempts to shape native metals, along with the development of processes for reducing ores, have been detected in Iran and in eastern and southern Turkey (at Çayönü and Asikli), from about the same time, the end of the 8th millennium BC. The ores used were copper oxides such as malachite, azurite, and cuprite, which, to be reduced, had to be heated to at least about 2120°F (1000°C), in a heat-resistant container with a reducing agent such as carbon monoxide, obtained by

Below: this pendant (late 4th millennium BC) comes from Susa, Persia (Iran). Laboratory analysis of the object demonstrated the oldest known "brazing" process: the ring attached to the dog's back was made from an alloy with a higher copper and silver content, which has a lower melting point than the elements that make up the gold object.

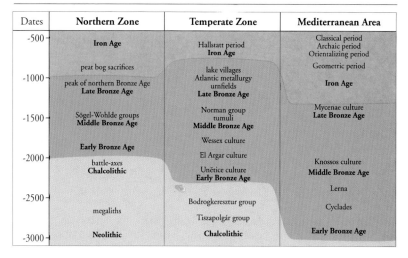

Dates	Northern Zone	Temperate Zone	Mediterranean Area
-500	**Iron Age**	Hallstatt period **Iron Age**	Classical period Archaic period Orientalizing period
-1000	peat bog sacrifices peak of northern Bronze Age **Late Bronze Age**	lake villages Atlantic metallurgy urnfields **Late Bronze Age**	Geometric period **Iron Age**
-1500	Sögel-Wohlde groups **Middle Bronze Age**	Norman group tumuli **Middle Bronze Age**	Mycenae culture **Late Bronze Age**
-2000	**Early Bronze Age** battle-axes **Chalcolithic**	Wessex culture El Argar culture Unětice culture **Early Bronze Age**	Knossos culture **Middle Bronze Age**
-2500	megaliths	Bodrogkeresztur group	Lerna Cyclades
-3000	**Neolithic**	Tiszapolgár group **Chalcolithic**	**Early Bronze Age**

burning wood. The nearly one hundred copper objects found at Çayönü and the forty-three copper beads set in a necklace found in the tombs of Asikli show that the Near East was ahead of western Europe, where the first metal objects did not appear until shortly before the 4th millennium BC.

The Balkans: precursors in Europe?

During the 6th millennium BC, southeastern and central Europe saw the rise of brilliant Chalcolithic civilizations that emerged from the local Neolithic Age, such as the culture of Karanovo V–VI (that is, of levels 5 and 6 of the archaeological site) and Gulmenitsa, among others. A large copper awl found in Balomir, Romania, dates from the early Neolithic (5900–5300). A bit later, in Greece, twelve sites showed copper objects and traces of metallurgical activity, including crucibles and debris. In Macedonia, for instance, at the site of Dikili Tash, archaeologists found the earliest remnants, a small series of very fine awls dating to about 5300 BC; other examples turned up in Thessaly, in Attica, and on the islands of Euboea, Keos, Crete, Naxos, and Chios.

The Copper Age, like those of bronze and of iron, did not occur simultaneously throughout Europe. In some cases the time gap extended to several centuries. But contacts between cultures or civilizations account for the appearance of similar phenomena from one region to another. This is one reason why the tripartite division is found everywhere, with a certain time lag from south to north.

The gold of Varna

The cemetery in Varna, Bulgaria, provides spectacular evidence of a goldsmithing activity that was flourishing as early as the second half of the 5th millennium. About 2,200 ornaments or elements of ornaments were found in graves during excavations that started in 1971, presenting to the world a civilization that had been unsuspected in Europe. The wealthiest persons were outfitted with gold diadems and scepters, along with extremely heavy axes with lateral blades made of copper, and even with spearheads, representing a considerable weight of metal. It must have come from the mines of Ai Bunar, near Stara Zagora, which even today yield green rocks rich in ores. From the beginning of the 5th millennium, ditches 33 to 66 feet (10 to 20 meters) deep and 13 to 16 feet (5 to 6 meters) wide were dug to allow miners to follow the deposits. The rock was probably heated and then cooled with water so that it would separate from the wall. The mines, mostly open to the sky, were supported by wooden stakes.

In the Tisza region of Hungary and Slovakia, between the 4th and 3rd millennia, the cultures of Tiszapolgár and then of Bodrogkeresztur, characterized by burials in the contracted position (usually on the side, with knees bent) in ditches or under tumuli, utilized copper tools and ornaments: very heavy axes and ax-hammers, beads, and spiral bracelets. Many amulets in copper and gold bore disklike designs, sometimes in anthropomorphic form.

The wealth of the grave goods, as well as the organization of certain settlements, including a palace, sanctuaries, shops, and perhaps the existence

This mask (left) executed in clay to capture the likeness of a man whose body was absent belongs to a set of three gravestones placed in the Varna necropolis on the coast of the Black Sea, excavated by I. Ivanov. The portrait carries ornaments of gold: a diadem on the forehead, convex disks at eye level, a plate surrounded by small gold nails to simulate the mouth decorated with incrustations. Opposite: a marble idol decorated with gold.

of an embryonic form of writing, testify to the brilliance of Chalcolithic civilization in southeastern Europe. The emergence of this civilization in Neolithic contexts contradicts the traditional view that it spread from the Near East or the Aegean and underscores the simultaneous flowering of metallurgical centers in several different regions.

Metallurgical centers appear in western Europe

In Corsica metallurgy first developed between the regions of Aleria and Sartène in the mid-4th millennium BC. At the site of Terrina, in particular, remains of crucibles and ovens were found not far from copper and chalcopyrite mines. That the crucibles' shape is similar to contemporaneous ones in Ozieri, Sardinia, and to somewhat later ones in Ledro, Trentino, demonstrates that several metal-working centers developed at the same time on both sides of the Alps. Whether situated in the area of St.-Véran (Hautes-Alpes, France), Trentino, or Aosta, they are characterized by proximity to the places where the ore was extracted and treated. Italy in the late 4th millennium saw the production of copper daggers and axes, found in the cemetery of Remedello (province of Verona). Farther north of the Alps, the Pfyn culture in Switzerland (between Lake Constance and Zurich), which produced beads, flat axes, and ingots, represents the western-most advance of the first metallurgy in central Europe in the 4th millennium.

In southern France, the regions of Quercy and Languedoc show the most advanced and diversified metallurgy. Copper, lead, and gold were processed there from the end of the Middle Neolithic. About 2500 BC a population concentrated in nearly 200

Equipped with large holes for attach- ment, this ornamental accessory 2¼ inches (6.5 centimeters) high depict- ing a bull (left) was discovered in the Varna necropolis. It probably decorated a dais, a tent, or an article of clothing of the departed. Com- posed of a thick layer of gold leaf, its entire periphery is studded with large dots in relief, created by means of the repoussé technique, probably made by punching the reverse side with an awl of bone or wood. Hammering gold into thick leaf is the basic technique used by the Varna goldsmiths and, in general, the first goldsmiths in Europe.

villages belonging to the Fontbouisse culture left very diversified material that revealed a strong interest in the local mineral wealth. The Roquefenestre site in Hérault included installations for grinding ore, tanks for washing, and areas for thermal treatment.

Daggers of finely worked flint or of copper, triangular in shape and affixed by small straps or thongs to halberds, are contemporaneous with the first signs of metallurgy in the Alpine region. Aside from decorative elements of shell, bone, and stone, daggers make up most of the grave goods from this tomb at Remedello (province of Brescia, Italy, left) dating from the early Chalcolithic (4th–3rd millennium BC). The deceased was placed in the contracted position.

The famous stela of the "tribal chief" (opposite, below) is the only engraved "movable" piece at the site of Mt. Bego. It is illustrated with the same kind of chipped-out daggers as the contemporaneous grave at Remedello, along with bulls' heads and a man struck in the head.

These first metallurgical products were depicted in cave art, demonstrating their high status. Thus, in the great sanctuary of rock art at Mt. Bego (Alpes-Maritimes, France) at an altitude of 9,240 feet (2,800 meters), triangular daggers similar to those of the Italian culture nearby at Remedello were incised in the rock by chipping. It is possible that the seasonal visits to this mountain site are linked to the activities of prospectors and migratory shepherds, which went on for centuries, until the Early Bronze Age, as can be seen in drawings of halberds and more elongated daggers dating to this period.

This unsuspected roaming in the mountains, starting in the 4th millennium and sometimes well before, was confirmed by the discovery of "Ötzi," the man of the Chalcolithic, who emerged in September 1991 from the Ötzal glacier on the Italian slope of the Tirolean Alps at an altitude of 10,600 feet (3,210 meters). The wealth of information supplied by Ötzi provides a unique glimpse of the life of a mountain man, which was abruptly interrupted one autumn day between 3300 and 3200 BC.

Two main valleys surround Mt. Bego: the Vallée des Merveilles and the valley of Fontanalba, at an altitude of more than 6,600 feet (2,000 meters). The carvings chipped into the gray-green or pink-coated schist surfaces were executed on rocks in the side of the mountain.

In southwestern Europe, the development of metallurgy was accompanied by the founding of fortified villages and citadels

In southwestern Europe—in Languedoc (the sites at Lebous and Boussargue) and especially in the southern Iberian Peninsula—where the first metallic objects appeared around 3000–2700 BC, a transformation of settlements can be seen.

The citadel of Los Millares, dominating the Andarax River from a height of 230 feet (70 meters), presents a complex

Chalcolithic Man

When first discovered in the Ötzal glacier, the man mummified by the ice had only his head and shoulders protruding from the fissure in which he was imprisoned. The force of glacial sliding had stripped him of his clothing and equipment, which were found nearby. Fairly short (5 feet 4 inches, or 1.6 meters), "Ötzi" bore tattoos on his back and joints (below, a detail). X rays revealed a body riddled with arthritis. He was dressed in a kind of skirt of softened leather, secured with a calfskin belt, goatskin thigh coverings held up by thongs, a shirt also of goatskin, and a wide cape made of knotted and woven swamp grasses. A bearskin hat and slippers stuffed with dried grasses and secured by netting completed his attire.

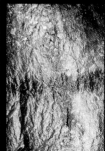

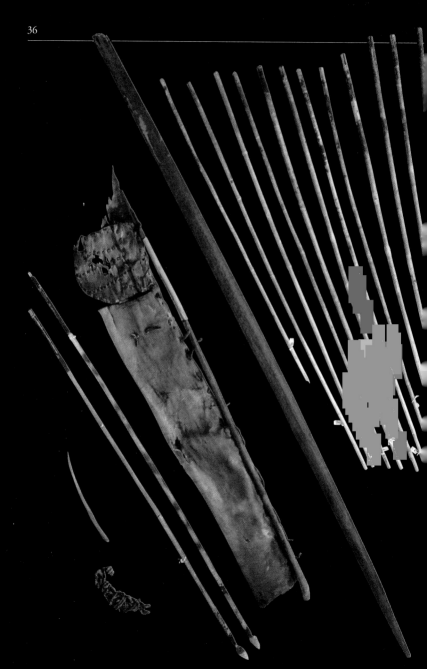

Ötzi's Outfit

Ötzi had set out with equipment typical of the hunter of his time: a flint dagger with an ash handle, inside a sheath of woven grasses (above and below, left); a sack; two birch-bark pails; an ax with a copper blade and a handle of yew wood (center); a bow 72 inches (1.8 meters) long, also of yew; and a leather quiver with fourteen arrows (opposite).

The bowstring, an awl, and four antler weapon tips completed the equipment. Below, a sketch of Ötzi's outfit and, at left, the grass netting that secured the slipper to his foot.

system of walls with four successive enclosures and semicircular towers that were excavated starting in 1897. Tombs of the *tholos* type (chamber dolmens with corbeled covering, inside a tumulus) associated with these walls contained arms made of copper—flat axes and daggers—alongside jewelry of amber, jadeite, variscite, turquoise, and even pendants of ostrich eggshell and African ivory. The tombs, like the citadel, are dated between 2400 and 2300 BC.

View of the fortified camp of Los Millares in Andalusia, Spain, with its sophisticated system of walls and its towers of unmortared stone (above).

Still farther to the west, the citadels of Vila Nova de São Pedro and of Zambujal, in the area of Lisbon, show that starting in the early 3rd millennium protection of the village was a cultural characteristic of the lower valley of the Tagus, seen also in the Lower Alentejo, the Algarve, the region of Huelva, Grenada, and Murcia. Graves, like the villages near them, often boasted sophisticated architecture. Some regional products, such as statuettes, pendants of marble, ivory, or bone, metallic jewelry, luxury ceramics, were of fine quality—all of which testify to a well-developed specialized craftsmanship.

It was long believed that the Chalcolithic Period in the Iberian Peninsula was the result of eastern influences. Recent analyses point instead to indigenous development. Groups that probably took advantage of local copper ore saw fit to erect walls for refuge or self-defense. In doing so, these societies inaugurated a new means of controlling wealth that would be one of the characteristics of the following period.

End of the Chalcolithic: toward a cultural unification of the European peoples

At the end of the Chalcolithic, Europe saw traces of cultures that developed ceramics associated with "typical" grave furnishings and practiced the new rite of individual burial. "Corded Ware" culture was so called because of the decoration applied by pressing cords around the necks of pots. These inhabitants provided some of the early copper articles, such as beads and axes. Corded pottery is associated with the rite of burial inside a mound and with grave furnishings that included a cup, an amphora, tools of flint and bone, and a (nonfunctional) battle-ax of hardstone. This culture covered northern central Europe, from Ukraine in the east to France and from Poland to Switzerland, with a strong concentration in Bohemia, and it seems to have had links with the Bell Beaker culture of central and western Europe.

In fact, between 2900 and 2500 BC, the pottery known as Bell Beaker ware appeared in many regions of Europe— the Iberian Peninsula, where it was studied very early, the

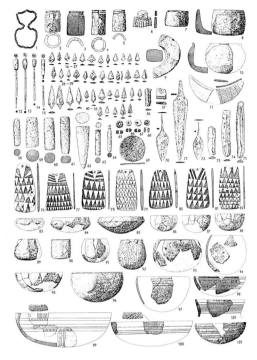

This plate, from a work by Hermann Müller-Karpe, presents typical objects from the Portuguese Chalcolithic Period. The drawing shows clearly the significant details of technique and decoration, while the layout helps elucidate the collection assembled by the archaeologist. Opposite: a model of one of the drawings, an idol in carved schist from Granza de Cespedes, 3rd millennium BC. Its head is represented by a triangle.

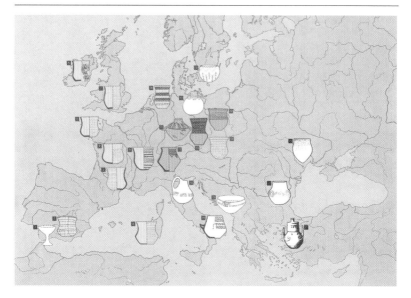

British Isles, Brittany, Belgium, the Netherlands, Germany, and Poland. These vessels, often decorated with rows of impressions made with reeds, were discovered in individual tombs of men alongside a small, tanged copper dagger (also called a Bell Beaker dagger), an archer's armband, slender flint arrows with wings or tangs, and V-shaped perforating studs. These graves are sometimes distinguished as well by small decorative elements of hammered gold, such as plaques or headbands.

The fact that these were individual graves—even if arranged within a collective burial site, as often occurs in the megalithic monuments of Brittany—and the stereotyped nature of the funerary material underline the particular social rank of these warriors. The distribution of Bell Beaker ware had previously inspired diffusionist theories that imagined migrations of "Bell Beaker peoples" from the region of the Tagus or the Guadalquivir Rivers, or possibly from central Europe—peddlers of amber or green rocks or copper prospectors swarming

This map shows the distribution of the various kinds of pottery that marked the first cultures to practice metallurgy in 3rd-millennium Europe: bell beakers (in yellow on the map), corded pottery (green), spherical amphoras, vases with funnel-shaped necks, and so on. The most widely diffused type is the bell beaker, found from central Europe to Spain and the British Isles. It was produced for several centuries. Corded ceramics are more common in central Europe.

across Europe. The current view, however, holds that this was a type of precious vessel intended for ritual use (possibly with beer) and left in certain tombs of minor warrior chiefs in the Chalcolithic.

Excavation of settlements, particularly in Portugal, confirms the presence of this pottery in the context of everyday life, at least within the fortified hill villages known as *castros,* erected since the dawn of the age of copper.

The Bronze Revolution

Bronze (an alloy of copper and tin) appeared between 3000 and 1500 BC in the eastern Mediterranean and in northern Europe. Initially it was used almost exclusively to make prestige objects (arms and jewelry). In fact, the Early Bronze Age in Europe seemed to be a continuation of the preceding period, relying on innovations already introduced then. Nevertheless, the new metal presented certain distinguishing characteristics. It was more resistant, more malleable, and more fusible than copper. Possession of bronze soon came to mark social differentiations that are reflected in grave furnishings. The alloy introduced greater complexity in the

Above: corded pottery from Cologne, Germany, dating from the 3rd millennium.

This late Bell Beaker piece (left) was discovered in a warrior's grave in Wiltshire, England. It is associated with typical equipment (below): a copper dagger, a short tanged arrowhead, and an archer's armband in schist.

A ceramic crucible found in the settlement of Fort-Harrouard (Eure-et-Loire, France) was subjected to laboratory analysis. Its successive layers of deposits showed that it had been used repeatedly to mix copper and tin to obtain bronze.

A bronze figurine from Enkomi, Cyprus, depicts a warrior wearing a horned helmet and brandishing a spear and shield. It stands on an ingot base shaped like an oxhide, symbolizing the mercantile wealth of Cyprus, the "isle of copper."

communities as well as tensions among groups that would lead to outbreaks of violence. Dense settlements seemed to become the rule.

Aegean palaces at the dawn of the Bronze Age

Some Chalcolithic structures can already be interpreted as prototypes of palaces, such as at Durankulak, Bulgaria, where a great building covered more than 1,700 square feet (160 square meters), or at level II of Troy (that is, the second of five Early Bronze Age cities built on the same site), in Anatolia, Turkey, where the dimensions of two *megarons* (Homeric term for a king's hall, the main room of a palace) seem to suggest two noble edifices, similar to other structures of the 3rd millennium in the region. At Lerna, in the Peloponnese, the "House of Tiles" was perhaps one of these prototypes conceived between 2500 and 2000 BC. Buildings that clearly loom above their neighbors are also prominent in Akoritika, near Kalamata, and Vasiliki in eastern Crete, where the maze of rooms and corridors suggests a palace.

The Early Bronze Age in Crete did not as yet see palaces as such. This was the early Minoan era

(3000–2100 BC). In the middle Minoan (2100–1700 BC), the construction of complex buildings within urban settlements that supplanted the rural communities marked an initial palace development. The architecture reflects the new power structure, concentrated in the hands of an elite. There are four known palaces (Phaistos, Knossos, Mallia, Zakro) from which Crete, now divided into small kingdoms, was apparently ruled.

These monumental palaces were organized around a central court, which was surrounded by functional quarters (storerooms, sanctuaries, ceremonial rooms). With the development of the centralized economy there appeared seal stones and the first form of writing based on hieroglyphics—not yet deciphered—which probably served to keep the palace accounts.

Ceramic production in Crete was prolific. At first polychrome, the vases were later executed on the potter's wheel and reached their peak in the style known as Kamares ware. This brilliant phase of civilization ended around 1700 BC with the destruction of the palaces for reasons—whether a natural catastrophe or an invasion—that remain unknown.

At the start of the middle Minoan era a veritable city grew up around the Palace of Phaistos, on the south shore of Crete over-looking the plain of Messara. Among the varied structures and workshops can be made out. With its typically Minoan layout, the building occupies a series of natural or artificial terraces. The first palace was destroyed at the end of the period and replaced by a second, with approximately the same floor plan. Its ruins, dating from the late Minoan era, can be seen here.

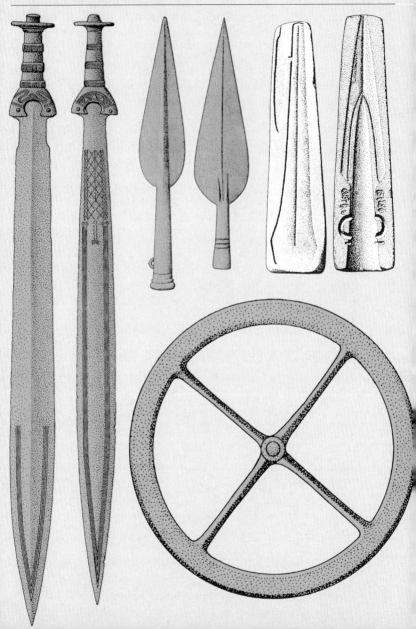

Copper is the basic metal of the Bronze Age. It can be poured into a mold; it is fusible. Cooled, it can change shape by means of hammering; it is malleable. It was put into circulation in the form of ingots. It was made into threads to line the edges of shields, which had to remain supple.

Classic bronze is 10 percent tin. Very fusible, it provides delicate castings; in hardened form, it can be brittle. It was used to make large swords, socketed spearheads, and wheels. Opposite, above, right: two-piece mold for a sword and socketed mold.

Mild bronze is 6 percent tin. It was hammered from ingots to obtain supple, resistant sheets, used to make vessels and, above all, arms and armor.

The second palace period in Crete

Destruction of the first palaces did not halt the development of Minoan civilization, which reached its full flowering at the end of the middle Minoan and the beginning of the late Minoan era (1700–1400 BC), at a time when western Europe was nearing the end of the Early Bronze Age. Like their predecessors, the second palaces served as political, religious, and economic centers, and their remains testify to their artistic distinction.

While following the structure of the earlier palaces, with living quarters surrounding a rectangular central courtyard oriented on the north-south axis, they expanded in size; Knossos, largest of them all, extended over 140,000 square feet (13,000 square meters).

The most striking innovation of this period was the development of fresco painting. The technique, which appeared at Knossos around 1600 BC, seems to have spread from there throughout Crete and the Cyclades. Religion doubtless predominated among the themes depicted, but the frescoes also show scenes of daily life. Their art exerted a considerable influence on the other arts, particularly on vase decoration, which henceforth took the form of black-figured decoration against a lighter background, dominated by floral and vegetal motifs.

The number of seal stones multiplied, and some of them depicted complex scenes.

Archives from this point on were written in Linear A, a writing that remains undeciphered.

Crete at this time played a dominant role among the islands; a Minoan thalassocracy, or maritime

Octopuses, dolphins, and fish appear frequently as motifs in Aegean art. The large amphora-shaped vase (left) found in a tomb at Prosymna (Argolid, 15th century BC) belongs to the tradition of ceramics decorated with marine themes from the mid-2nd millennium. Along the Mediterranean coastline, fishing holds a major place in the economy and in daily life.

The acrobat from the Palace of Knossos (left) was no doubt depicted participating in a bullfighting game. He is shown flinging himself onto the bull's back. The ivory statuette echoes the gestures and movements of figures in the frescoes at Knossos and Tiryns.

To reconstruct the interior of the palace of Knossos, Arthur Evans did not hesitate to use concrete, bricks, and metal girders. Though often criticized, the reconstructed elevation of the buildings with their bright coloring conveys a sense of the Minoans' decorative refinements.

dominion, has been proposed, as reflected in the adoption of many aspects of Minoan art in the Cyclades. It held sway until the volcanic eruption of Thera about 1500 BC and the new, brutal destruction of the Minoan cities by fire. It is still not certain, moreover, whether this destruction was linked to the natural catastrophe or instead to Mycenaean invasions. Whatever the cause, a century later Crete was depopulated. One palace continued to function, that of Knossos, probably under Mycenaean occupation. Its archives were kept in a third written language, Linear B, which has been decoded and identified as a primitive form of Greek. Linear B is also found on the tablets at Pylos and Mycenae, confirming the hypothesis of a Mycenaean conquest of Crete.

With the destruction of the second palaces, Minoan civilization, the principal power in the Aegean from 2100 to 1400, disappeared, replaced for a time by the power of Mycenae.

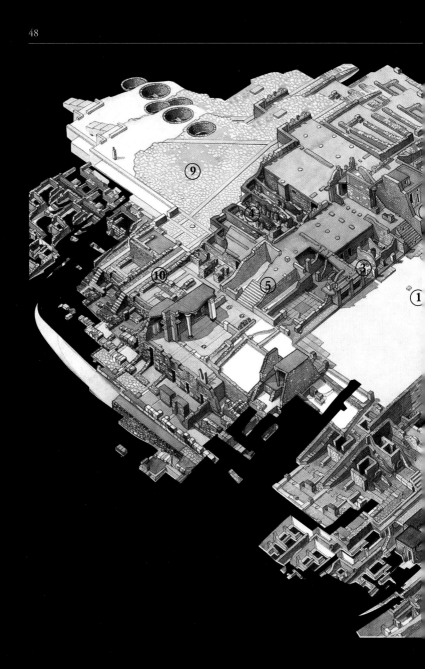

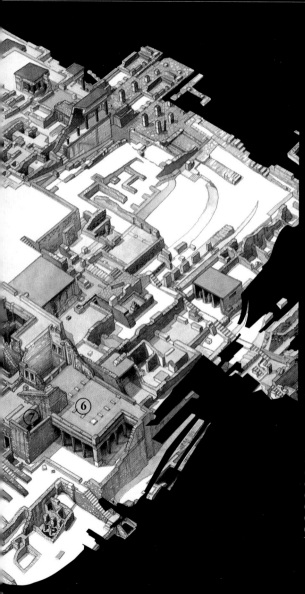

The Palace of Minos

Beginning in the middle Minoan era, a true city developed at Knossos. A palace arose whose ruins were covered over by those of the succeeding period. In the late Minoan era, the urban area extended over a few hundred hectares (400 or 500 acres) and the buildings were greatly dispersed. The town plan was not clear, but the palace itself was much better known: consisting of four wings arranged around a central rectangular courtyard, it included hundreds of rooms divided up among five floors. The plan is labyrinthine, but the rooms form coherent units (royal apartments, domestic quarters, artisans' studios, storerooms); the most important are listed below. Frescoes (such as the bullfighting scene on the following pages) decorated many walls.

(1) central courtyard
(2) throne room
(3) sanctuaries
(4) storerooms
(5) south propylaeum (vestibule or entrance)
(6) hall of the double axes
(7) queen's *megaron* (main hall)
(8) grand staircase
(9) west court
(10) procession corridor

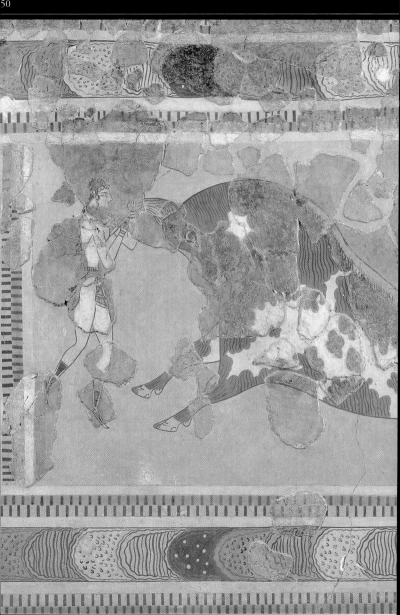

Between East and West: the Mediterranean islands

A homogeneous culture spread throughout the eastern Mediterranean during the second half of the 3rd millennium BC. The inclusion of Cyprus in Mediterranean routes—it was in contact at the time with Anatolia and Crete—was no doubt due to the exploitation of its rich copper deposits. The island's urbanization between the 4th and the 3rd millennia was reflected in the existence of cult buildings known primarily from miniature terra-cotta depictions.

The islands of the western Mediterranean also reflected Aegean influences and, gradually, became points of contact with the Atlantic world. Systems of walls with circular towers were found in the settlement of Castellucio in Sicily. Later, in Sardinia, large towers surrounded by structures of stone terraces known as *nuraghi* arose.

Polished marble idols dated between 2700 and 2000 BC were diffused throughout the Cyclades. At left is one of the oldest of such statuettes, found at Chalandriani. They varied in height, from 4 inches to 5 feet (10 centimeters to 1.5 meters), and identification is sometimes possible, not of their sculptors but at least of the studios that produced them. These works bear the first hints of something approaching a signature.

This curious bowl (below), dated 2100–2000 BC, was found at Vounous, Cyprus. It shows a sanctuary within an enclosing wall, its entrance crowned by a large lintel. Inside, human figures and bulls take part in a ceremony, possibly a sacrifice.

The Iberian Peninsula in the Early Bronze Age was dominated by El Argar civilization

In the southern Iberian Peninsula, following the Bell Beaker culture, the early 2nd millennium BC brought an increase in individual burial, the development of metallurgy, and a clear tendency to urbanization, especially between Murcia and Grenada, where El Argar culture was spreading, comprising a number of fortified settlements. At first copper and gold were worked, followed very quickly by silver (a unique development at the time) and bronze, in specialized centers producing magnificent prestige articles that were arranged in tombs.

Around 2000 BC the citadel of Fuente Alamo (Almeria province) included a set of massive rectangular buildings that seem to have been consolidated several times; reinforcements of the walls reached a considerable thickness (between 6½ and 10 feet, or 2 to 3 meters).

The site of El Argar, situated 8 miles (12 kilometers) from the sea on a terrace 100 feet (30 meters) above the Antas River, is the best known. It became famous for its remains of fortifications, houses, traces of bronze-working studios, and especially for its one thousand tombs.

The dead of El Argar were buried in dwellings as well as in a cemetery. The bodies were buried in ditches, in stone chests, under the floors of houses, or even within the thicknesses of some walls. In a second phase, beginning in

Sword handles plated with gold leaf (this sword is from the El Argar culture, found at Guadalajara) are relatively rare in Europe during the Bronze Age. In the Mycenaean and Nordic worlds, above all, such handles adorn weapons deposited in the tombs of wealthy warriors. Here, the very malleable gold leaf has been applied by pressure on a decoration already prepared in relief on the base. In other cases, the gold leaf is decorated beforehand by stamping and then secured by mechanical means to the wooden or bronze base of the handle.

1700 BC, the custom arose of placing the dead in contracted position in large jars, or *pithoi*. Men were accompanied by daggers and halberds, while women displayed bracelets, pendants, necklaces, and brooch-like attachments. Higher-ranking women bore a fine diadem of beaten gold or silver, ring-type jewelry of precious metals, as well as a small copper knife. Throughout this period, from 2000 to 1600, many tombs of important individuals were observed throughout the El Argar territory of southeastern Spain, at Fuente Alamo, El Oficio, Gatas, and so on. Double graves for a man and a woman were common. Excavations in several villages of the region have provided valuable information on this original culture. Its new structures, for instance, did not impede the growth of farming, which continued to dominate the economy, probably due to the creation of irrigation systems.

Gold and silver diadems, copper and bronze daggers, and bracelets and pendants of gold, silver, or copper demonstrate the abundance of the metals exploited in the early 2nd millennium BC. This typological sketch (below) from the El Argar necropolis also shows a *pithos*, or funerary urn.

An Atlantic community

In the western Iberian Peninsula, a particular cultural region developed in Portugal that also featured fortified settlements and necropolises with individual tombs surrounded by small circular walls, such as in Atalaia. These latter represent transitional rites between the cultures of the Mediterranean and the Atlantic.

Some of the excavated objects—such as the flat axes, daggers, and points (knives or weapon tips) from Palmela of arsenical copper—suggest that the Portuguese settlements

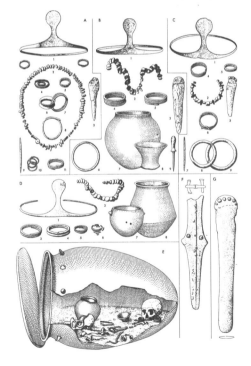

belonged primarily to cultures developed along the Atlantic, from north to south, or at least that they must have maintained frequent exchanges with the Atlantic cultures. The tomb of Quinta da Agua Branca provides an example of hybrid influences, with the presence of a long, tanged dagger that recalls those of Carnoët in Brittany, as well as a wide diadem of beaten gold.

One particular type of gold necklace is found from Portugal to Brittany: the *gargantilla,* a high collar made of gold leaf cut horizontally toward the front. Other objects are common to the cultural bloc along the Atlantic, such as arsenical copper halberds or, a truly exceptional product, lunulae. These large, flat, crescent-shaped votive necklaces of very finely beaten gold are primarily seen in the British Isles but also have been found in Brittany and Denmark. One Portuguese example came to light in Cabaceiros de Basto, alongside two gold-leaf disks of a kind also found in Great Britain.

Princes of Armorica and Wessex

Between 1900 and 1500 BC both sides of the English Channel shared the same cultural community, to judge from the fine offerings left in tumulus graves.

The Bush Barrow, a mound erected near Stonehenge, is contemporary with the

The figure curled up in this reconstruction of a *pithos* tomb from El Argar wears a diadem of precious metal.

This lunula, or crescent necklace, from the treasure of Bourbriac (Côtes-d'Armor, France), 2000–1600 BC, belongs to a very widespread type, decorated with incised designs—here, continuous and zigzagging lines along the edges of the piece. The finest examples, from Ireland, feature the most delicate decoration on fragile sheets of finely hammered metal.

final phase of the use of that "solar temple." The barrow contained daggers and axes with small bronze borders, sheet-gold plaques sewn onto clothing, and a scepter consisting of polished stone with a rod decorated with details in gold, bone, and ivory, symbolizing power.

The wealth of the grave goods explains why these have been called "princely" civilizations. Their tumuli contained ceremonial weapons, jewelry of bronze, gold, and even amber, hardstones, or jet, and gold or silver vessels. The dwellings of these minor princes both in Dorset and in the region of Berrien (in Finistère, France) seem linked to trading activity against a backdrop of rural pastoral economies.

It can be assumed that the deposits of tin, required to make the new alloy, bronze—and exploited in the form of cassiterite in British Cornwall and Brittany— may explain the wealth of the princes of Wessex and probably also of Armorica (Brittany). Moreover, possession of this precious metal, almost totally absent from the Mediterranean basin, promoted exchanges with the East. Beads of blue molten glass found in Armorica that greatly resemble Egyptian products from Tell al-Amarna

The tumulus of St.-Fiacre in Morbihan, France (above), contained the tomb of a so-called Armorican prince, who was buried with precious furnishings, particularly the remains of a small silver goblet. The cup shown below (18th–17th century BC), cut from a block of amber, was found in a tomb in Hove, Sussex. In the Early Bronze Age, such ceremonial vessels, sometimes in amber but more often in gold or silver, accompanied the deceased.

(1800–1400 BC) partially explain the hypothesis of direct relations between the eastern Mediterranean and western Europe. Analysis of the beads has shown that the western examples were in fact produced locally. It remains striking, however, that the Egyptian style could be found as far west as the British Isles.

The tumuli of Wessex and Armorica, contemporary with the late phases of Stonehenge, which saw the erection of its most monumental elements, seemed for some time to be the result of influences from Mycenae because of the status they carried and the presence of similar kinds of amber jewelry, glass beads, and gold dishes. Dating with carbon 14, however, has proved that the western tombs are older by several centuries.

Dagger blades or short swords of arsenical copper or bronze, decorated with incised lines following the blade edges, as well as low-flanged axes were among the grave goods from 2000–1600 BC brought to light in the tumulus at La Motta, near Lannion, Brittany.

Cultural impact of a metallurgical center: Unĕtice

Central Europe was a true crossroads, benefiting from the proximity of rich ore in the regions of the Alps and the Carpathians. It became the home of brilliant cultures, foremost among them Unĕtice, the product of Corded Ware and Bell Beaker cultures.

Also found in this chieftain's grave were many finely shaped flint arrowheads along with a parallel-sided pendant covered with thick gold leaf.

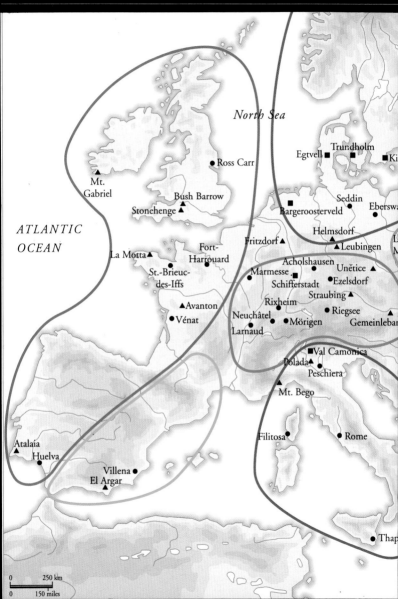

North Sea

Egtvell ■ Trundholm ■ ■ ■ Ki

Ross Carr ●

Mt. Gabriel ▲

ATLANTIC OCEAN

Bush Barrow ▲
Stonehenge ▲

Seddin ●
Bargeroosterveld ■
Eberswa ●

La Motta ▲
St.-Brieuc-des-Iffs ●

Fort-Hartouard

Fritzdorf ▲
Helmsdorf ▲
Leubingen ▲
L... M...

Acholshausen ●
Marmesse ■
Schifferstadt ●
Rixheim ●
Neuchâtel ●
Larnaud
Mörigen ●

Unětice ▲
Ezelsdorf ●
Straubing ▲
Riegsee ●
Gemeinleban

Avanton ▲
Vénat ●

Val Camonica ■
Polada ▲
Peschiera ●

Mt. Bego ●

Atalaia ▲
Huelva ●

Villena ●
El Argar ▲

Filitosa ●

Rome ●

Thap ●

0 ___ 250 km
0 ___ 150 miles

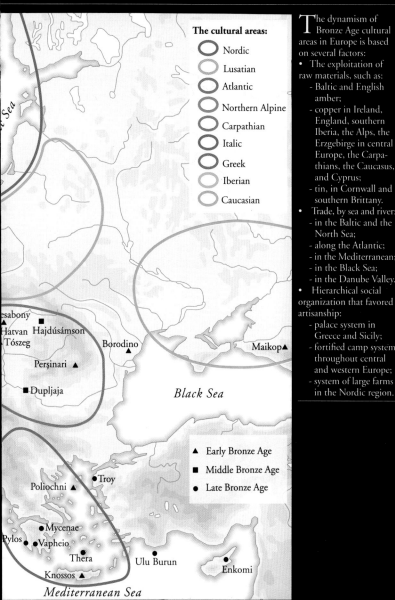

The cultural areas:

- Nordic
- Lusatian
- Atlantic
- Northern Alpine
- Carpathian
- Italic
- Greek
- Iberian
- Caucasian

The dynamism of Bronze Age cultural areas in Europe is based on several factors:
- The exploitation of raw materials, such as:
  - Baltic and English amber;
  - copper in Ireland, England, southern Iberia, the Alps, the Erzgebirge in central Europe, the Carpathians, the Caucasus, and Cyprus;
  - tin, in Cornwall and southern Brittany.
- Trade, by sea and river:
  - in the Baltic and the North Sea;
  - along the Atlantic;
  - in the Mediterranean;
  - in the Black Sea;
  - in the Danube Valley.
- Hierarchical social organization that favored artisanship:
  - palace system in Greece and Sicily;
  - fortified camp system throughout central and western Europe;
  - system of large farms in the Nordic region.

t Sea

Ősabony
Hatvan Hajdúsámson
Tószeg
Borodino
Perşinari ▲
Maikop ▲
■ Dupljaja

Black Sea

▲ Early Bronze Age
■ Middle Bronze Age
● Late Bronze Age

Poliochni ▲   ● Troy

● Mycenae
Pylos ●
● Vapheio
Thera ●   Ulu Burun ●   Enkomi ●
Knossos ▲

Mediterranean Sea

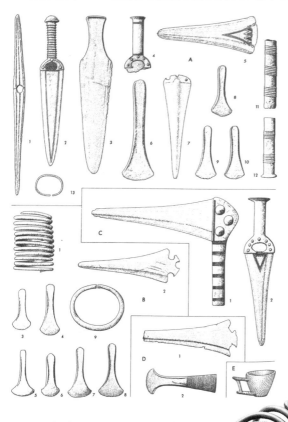

Daggers, halberds, axes, and bracelets made by the Unětice culture are found in the hoards of central Germany (typological sketch at left).

Below: this thick gold bracelet, decorated with incised lines at both ends, as well as several coiled gold wires that may have been used either as jewelry or types of ingots, are from the hoard of Heidolsheim in Alsace from the early 2nd millennium BC.

Situated a few miles northwest of Prague, the site of Unětice features a cemetery with some sixty flat tombs dating from 2200 to 1800 BC. Its grave goods include triangular-blade daggers, diverse and abundant jewelry, especially in women's graves, and a great variety of pottery, such as cups with low carination, or keel (the ridge where top and bottom parts are attached), jars, and miniature vases.

Uněticeʹs plentiful supply of metal products allowed the residents to accumulate reserves, which resulted in numerous hoards of ingots in the shape of torques (metal collars or neck rings, also known as ring ingots), daggers, axes, and other material. Some objects from this cultural and metallurgical center, such as eyelet fibulae and torques with terminal scrolls, were exported, primarily throughout Slovakia, Moravia, Bohemia, Saxony, and Silesia. Its settlements were fortified or open on river embankments and clearly included "streets," or pathways for circulation. Cemeteries built outside the villages generally enclosed some fifty flat tombs in which the dead were placed on their right side with legs bent up.

B uilt with a circular or rectangular floor plan, the houses of Bronze Age central Europe had a skeleton of poles covered with mud walls and a thatched roof (above, reconstruction in the archaeological park of Asparn an der Zaya, Austria). Smoke from a central fireplace could escape through the roof. The family formed the residential unit. Hamlets, widely dispersed, also had barns and stables. The population concentrated in strategic spots, which were then fortified.

Tells of the Tisza Valley

A vestige of the original settlement in the basin of the Carpathians and its neighboring area to the south, the tell of the Chalcolithic tradition is an artificial mound presenting the remains of successive settlements, one on top of the other. The houses (consisting of a wooden structure covered with mud or branches, sometimes logs) were rebuilt on top of one another, while the layout of the residences and streets remained unchanged. Tells offer an accumulation of many feet of archaeological deposits and thus represent an essential source of information on the Bronze Age in these regions. Moreover, they reveal much about a stable habitation based on a society of farmers and herders.

Several cultures present this kind of tell settlement combined with others in the form of fortified caves. All these cultures also had fine ceramics decorated with embossments, flutings, and incrustations of white paste. Kisapostag culture, for instance, named for a cemetery of 1,600 tombs, also known as Nagyrév-

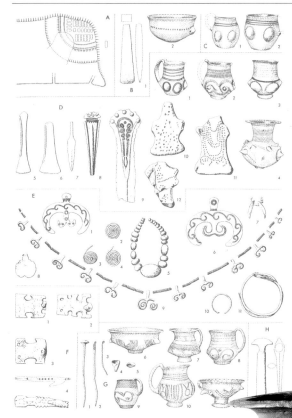

Ceramicists of central Europe achieved a certain exuberance. The ceramic vase from Barca, near Bratislava (below and at left, in a typological sketch), made of high-fired and glazed clay, is decorated with relief motifs resembling nipples.

Hatvan culture, showed such characteristic elements as a two-handled vase recalling the Aegean and Anatolian cantharus; vases with white incrustations on polished black background; massive axes with lateral handles; and long daggers with a metallic handle decorated with incised spirals. Decorative elements of harnesses (bits and hames) bear witness to the importance of the horse at that time, used as a mount.

Local cultures grouped around Unětice

can be related through their use of similar techniques, distinguished through their innovative forms. In Bavaria, Straubing-Singen culture is characterized primarily by hammered copper objects, such as fibulae with large, flat, circular heads; large tubular beads; and rimmed axes with rounded blade. Axes of the same type as well as elongated ones called spatulate axes are found in Switzerland around Lake Constance, which accommodated lakeside dwellings arranged on wooden platforms near the waterside.

The "sheet-metal group"

The culture of the Rhône River has been located in the Valais district and the canton of Vaud in Switzerland, in eastern France, and on the plains of the Saône River. It produced objects of hammered copper (fibulae with trefoil or circular heads), as well as spatulate axes and metal-hilted daggers richly decorated with geometric fluting. Earthenware pitchers and jars decorated with large relief cords typify its pottery.

   Farther north, in Alsace and the Rhine valley, Adlerberg culture offers some variants, such as round-bellied pots decorated with copper elements that are again hammered, a feature that led Swiss archaeologist E. Vogt to place all these cultures under the name *Blechkreis,* or "sheet-metal group." The settlements are either dispersed and open or concentrated and fortified. Coffer tombs are common.

Italy's first cultures

In northern Italy, a widespread culture known as Polada occupied Lombardy, Veneto, and Trentino from the late 3rd to the mid-2nd millennium BC. Numerous sites with settlements were concentrated on the shores of the lakes of Varese, Iseo, and Ledro. Others were found in the swampy areas of Trentino. The lakeside

This "Rhône dagger" with metal handle from the hoard of the Taburles in the Hautes-Alpes, France, is very finely decorated with a motif of hatched triangles, zigzags, and other geometric shapes at the top of the blade and handle. X rays revealed that the hollow handle is secured to the blade by seven rivets.

settlements, formerly called lake villages, were in fact built not on lakes, as supposed, but in nearby wetlands.

Typical pottery includes low cups with handles that might be nose-shaped, thumb-shaped (*ad ascia*), or crescent-shaped (*ansa lunata*). Metal objects (weapons and fibulae) recall forms known in the Rhône or Straubing cultures and in Unĕtice culture. In Emilia, northern Italy, between the Po and the Apennines, a type of settlement gave its name to a culture that developed particularly in the Early Bronze Age, the *terramare,* a name designating the piles of dark earth that accumulated following the reconstruction of wooden settlements. Built by farmers and herders, these villages, often erected along rivers, disappeared at the beginning of the Late Bronze Age. They produced an original metallurgy, typified by the fibula, an ancient "safety pin," generally decorated, used to adjust or fasten the ample flowing clothing of antiquity.

Apennine culture from central to southern Italy, in the mountainous countryside, is characterized by cave settlements in which we also find ceramic vases with a handle rising up in the shape of a horn.

About fifty anthropomorphic stelae of the Lunigiana type were found in eastern Liguria, Italy, in the region of Garfagnana, concentrated particularly on the left slope of the valley of the Magra. Some of these stelae date from the Iron Age, but most range from the Chalcolithic to the late Bronze Age. They are of two main types. The Pontevecchio type resembles the statuemenhirs on which the head has not been separated from the body. This type, however, already has the design of a triangular-blade dagger carved into the stone. The stela at left, found at Minucciano, belongs to the Filetto-Malgrate group. The figure, with head well set off, is also armed with a dagger, its handle visible.

This bronze dagger from Lake Ledro (Trentino), belonging to the Polada culture, has a blade decorated with incised lines and a handle with metallic elements meant to hold circular bits of organic material (possibly wood, bone, and horn). The weapon is found in the typological sketch presented by Müller-Karpe (below, the top left item). Numerous objects for domestic use illustrated in the sketch, such as large pins, or fibulae, with hammered circular head or trefoil, recall products of the "sheet-metal group."

The Mycenaean world, consigned to oblivion until the excavations of its great sites brought to light its grandiose architecture and refined craftsmanship, symbolized the pinnacle of the Bronze Age in the mid-2nd millennium. Nevertheless, even the glory of Greece could not eclipse those other civilizations—every bit as remarkable—that left their mark elsewhere in Europe.

CHAPTER 3

MYCENAEANS IN THE HEART OF EUROPE?

The irrefutable identification of Mycenae was made from this site first of all (at left, the Lion Gate, c. 1250 BC), from the treasures (right, a gold mask dating from the 16th century BC), and finally from the tablets inscribed in Linear B, which mention its name.

At the end of the middle Helladic era (between 1700 and 1600 BC), the Achaeans (or Mycenaeans) from the southern part of mainland Greece began to establish an economic center and a dynamic culture, influenced by frequent trading with Crete and the Cyclades, whose products they copied. The destruction of Cretan settlements (around the time of, if not caused by, the eruption of Thera in the 16th century BC) paved the way for the advent of the Mycenaeans. In the following century, they came to dominate the Aegean, where the Bronze Age reached its peak; this was the late Helladic era, which began in about 1600 and ended about 1100 BC.

Built on a rocky spur, Mycenae adapted to its topography. Below, the palace (in the middle) and the fortified town. The entrance and the Lion Gate are at the right, toward the northwest, near Circle A of the tombs, within the walls. Mycenae is one of the first European cities recognized by inscriptions found at the site itself.

The Mycenaeans, or the Age of Heroes

The excavations in Mycenae unearthed the history of princes who had spoken an archaic form of Greek and lived in fortified palaces. From 1600 BC these princes were buried with sumptuous offerings, including gold masks associated with heroic stature. The Trojan War, about 1300 BC, attests to the first colonial expansion of the Mycenaeans, in the eastern Mediterranean.

The region occupied by the Mycenaeans, at the junction of two major routes to the Peloponnese, as well as the rest of the southern Greek mainland became cultural hubs characterized by palatial and later urban organization, truly monumental art, and a system of writing. Nowhere else in Greece have treasures to rival those of Mycenae been found. The perfectly intact tombs of Circle A, discovered by Heinrich Schliemann in 1876, and those of Circle B, discovered in 1951 and excavated by John Papadimitriou, George Mylonas, and others, mark it as the key city of the era that gave birth to the traditions and history of Greece. Archaeological relics trace its existence from prehistoric times to this period of hegemony, an Age of Heroes, as the Greek historian Thucydides, who lived in the 5th century BC, would describe it much later.

The monumental remains are mainly to be found in Thessaly and the Peloponnese. The greatest palaces were built in Mycenae, Tiryns, Pylos, Athens, and Thebes. The list of cities Homer cites as having sent ships to the Trojan War (*Iliad,* 2:484–877) reflects the large number of small political units that belonged to the same community.

"Beautiful Mycenae" was undoubtedly one of the most important among them, noted for its architectural monuments such as the "Treasury of Atreus" (a *tholos,* or round, corbel-vaulted tomb) and the Lion Gate at the acropolis, where the remains of the Palace of Atreus still stand, surrounded by its mighty ramparts. Pylos, in the fertile area of Messenia, is another prominent city, notable for Nestor's palace. When excavated by Carl Blegen, the palace yielded important archives in a form of Linear B of exactly the same type as documents at Knossos.

The Treasury of Atreus, c. 1250 BC, is one of the most impressive monuments in Mycenae. Its corbeled vault is 44 feet (13.5 meters) high and its facade was initially embellished with two sculpted and painted columns, now on exhibit in the British Museum in London. Some have seen such tombs—mistakenly—as the origin of certain influences on the vaulted tombs of west European megalithic structures, which, according to carbon 14 tests, actually predate Mycenaean tombs by some three thousand years.

Royal tombs keep watch on the Argolid

From the heights of Mycenae one can see the vast expanse of the Argolid, which is dominated by the fortified city. Within the walls, abutting them, was Circle A of the royal tombs (prominently visible in this photograph). This circle was lined with large, vertical slabs. Discovered by Schliemann in 1876, the five shaft graves contained a treasure trove of gold offerings dating from about 1600 to 1500 BC. In addition to the five masks of the bodies buried within, the inventory of discoveries included ornate swords encrusted with gold decoration, dishes, plaques and a crown embellished by concentric gold circles, a seal stone made of sardonyx, amber necklaces, a silver rhyton in the shape of a muzzled bull's head, a diadem, and gold horns. A stela of sculpted stone, decorated with spirals toward its top, depicts a chariot race. Southwest of the walled city a second series of "royal" tombs, called Circle B, used from 1650 to 1550 BC, was excavated between 1952 and 1954.

The "Mask of Agamemnon"

For Schliemann this mortuary mask proved a revelation: the treasure could only have belonged to a celebrated man—Agamemnon himself, king of Argos and Mycenae. Although Homer records his essential role in the Trojan War, no direct archaeological evidence of his existence has been found. Indeed, identification of this individual is problematic, since the gold mask dates to 1600 BC, two or three centuries before the Trojan War, when Agamemnon lived. The corpse in Grave V, buried with a death mask—perhaps in imitation of the pharaohs—was, in any event, a person of rank. Four other repoussé gold masks were placed on the faces of individuals buried in the royal cemetery of Circle A. Only one tomb in Circle B contains a mask, possibly older than the others. It is made of a natural alloy of gold and silver called electrum.

The commercial networks of Mycenae

Most Mycenaean products of the 16th and 15th centuries BC seem comparable to Cretan models, possibly derived from them. This is true of seal stones decorated with intaglios, great bronze vessels, gold and silver goblets, and especially frescoes. In the 14th century, Mycenaean expansion is widely attested in the Aegean world and beyond: products are found at Troy and on the Syrian and Palestinian coasts. First Miletus, then Cyprus was colonized; in the western Mediterranean, Mycenaean trading posts were set up in southern Italy, Sicily, and, farther north, in the Balkans. Returning ships brought luxury products from Egypt and the Levant back to Mycenaean Greece.

In 1982 a shipwreck from the 14th century BC was discovered off Ulu Burun, near Kaş on the southern coast of Turkey, at a depth between 140 and 200 feet (43 to 60 meters). Excavated between 1984 and 1994, it brought to light thousands of objects and furnished valuable information on commercial traffic in the Mediterranean during the Bronze Age. The cargo

In the 16th century BC the island of Thera (Thíra) in the Cyclades was a highly active port (below, a mural found at the site of Akrotiri). It had three-story houses embellished with colonnades and boasting windows. The boats shown are propelled either by sail or by oars. The raised prow is not typical of the Mediterranean but is characteristic of boats found in Scandinavian rock carvings.

included more than 10 tons of copper in the form of 354 ingots of the "oxhide" type, unquestionably from Cyprus, and about a ton of ingots and various objects of tin, of indeterminate origin. Among the pottery, Canaanite jars manufactured in Palestine or Syria (Canaan) held various materials: resin and turpentine, olives, glass beads, orpiment (a reddish coloring agent containing arsenic). The ship had carried such exotic products as a supply of ebony from southern Egypt, amber beads from the Baltic, ivory from elephant and hippopotamus tusks, most likely from the eastern Mediterranean, and shells of ostrich eggs from North Africa or Syria. It contained bronze tools and weapons of Egyptian, Levantine, and Mycenaean types. Among other important pieces were several Assyrian, Cassite, and Syrian cylindrical seal stones, a glass ingot, a gold cup, and silver and gold jewelry, including a scarab piece inscribed with the name Nefertiti.

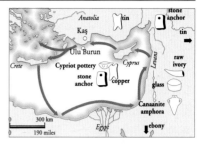

The Mycenaean civilization, parallel to its borrowings from Minoan traditions, demonstrated a fund of originality as well: a cyclopean architecture, that is, employing large, irregular stone blocks without mortar, and a form of writing, Linear B, which, through the tablets of Knossos and Pylos, provides ample information on the socioeconomic organization of the small kingdoms of the period, with their female textile workers, their metallurgists, their soldiers, and their tax officials. Mycenae produced ceramics of its own typical style: amphoras, beaked pitchers, rhytons, jars, and cups with double handles. The decoration consisted of dark motifs, usually floral, on a light background, which made its way to the trading posts of Thessaly,

The cargo of the ship-wreck of Ulu Burun confirmed the links between the Egyptians (below, the Nefertiti scarab), the countries of the Near East, Cyprus, and the Mycenaeans. It can be assumed that the boat, which departed from the Levantine coast, had put in at Cyprus before approaching the Turkish coast, Crete, and possibly stopping at the Mycenaean sites of Greece, or even at trading posts farther to the northwest. Then it may have headed back down to the coast of North Africa, toward the Nile Delta, and ended up in Phoenicia (map above).

old man

vase

weapons

gold

young girl

Macedonia, Albania, Italy, and as far as Sicily—in the Palace of Thapsos—as well as Cyprus and Lebanon, all of which represent stations in a Mycenaean thalassocracy (or sea empire), seven or eight centuries before that of Magna Graecia.

"Tumulus culture" of central Europe

How far did the Mycenaean sphere extend? Was it compatible with other dynamic and independent cultural zones in Europe? The question asked by archaeologists was summarized by Colin Renfrew in the formulation "Is Stonehenge possible without Mycenae?" in an article published in 1968.

The culture of Stonehenge was marked by tumuli, spectacular funeral forms in the landscape. So characteristic of the Early and Middle Bronze Age are these burial mounds that they inspired the notion of the "Tumulus cultures," which extend through central Europe as far as Alsace (Haguenau culture). The tradition of the mound goes back to the Chalcolithic Period, with the famous tumulus of Maikop in the northern Caucasus. In the Early Bronze Age, the tumulus of Leubingen (Germany), a mound 26 feet (8 meters) high and 110 feet (34 meters) in diameter covers a chamber constructed from a double row of sloping vertical logs. The body of an elderly man was laid out along the axis of the tomb and an adolescent was placed across him perpendicularly—possibly a young woman, to judge from the gold ornamentation found among the offerings.

Such tombs contained metal objects, from weapons— including a sword with metallic handle and daggers—to jewelry, for example, brooches with small wheeled heads or eyelets and toe rings. Through their style, as well as that of the funeral vases, a number of local cultures could be identified and distinguished.

The Tumulus culture of central Europe corresponds to a prosperous phase that is found in the successive

The aristocratic nature of central and northern European society in the mid-2nd millennium is seen particularly in the tumulus graves. A funerary mound contained at its center one or two chambers built of logs or flat stones (opposite page, above, the tumulus of Pitten reconstructed in the open-air museum of Asparn, Austria). The grave might contain rich offerings, as at Leubingen, Germany (opposite page, below), with high-status weapons for men and jewels, including pins (above), for women.

settlements forming the tells, like one at Tószeg, Hungary, with its family houses and range of ceramic products: saucers, fish plates, portable fireplaces, miniature altars, idols, model chariots, baby bottles, rattles, animal statuettes, and so on. Small objects made from bone or antler that might belong to elements of a horse harness carry incised spiral motifs that recall certain Mycenaean motifs, in particular those figuring on metallic sword handles. These indicate cultural similarities.

The tumuli of Jutland are fascinating for the impressive preservation of organic remains of the departed, as well as of their clothing and the offerings, thanks to the impregnation of oak coffins with tannin.

Jutland's impressive tombs and Nordic dynamism

Tumuli were also built in Denmark's Jutland, around 1400 BC. These mounds, measuring 10 to 13 feet (3 to 4 meters) high and 66 feet (20 meters) in diameter, covered stone coffers or oak coffins made of a section of trunk split in two and hollowed out by an ax and through burning. Tannin has preserved the textiles and felt of clothing. The variety and elegance of the latter confirms the impression of luxury given by jewelry and armor of bronze.

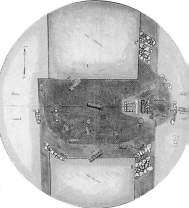

One of the most famous coffins contained the young girl of Egtved, found in 1921. She was wrapped in a steer hide. The acidity of the soil, while it dissolved the calcium of her bones, preserved her long hair, skin, fingernails, and the enamel of her teeth, leaving her appearance intact. The young girl wore a linen bodice with half-length sleeves; the short skirt was formed of a series of linen strings attached to a sash wound twice around the waist. On her feet she wore linen slippers. Her jewelry consisted of bronze bracelets and a large disk decorated with spirals attached at the waist, as well as a bone comb. She was buried with a small sack containing the incinerated bones of a child eight years of age and two small birch-bark containers, one with a linen rope, a hair ribbon, and an awl, and the other some powder, the remains of a drink derived from

Above: a watercolor of a tumulus grave in Borum Eshoj, by J. Magnus Petersen; at center, the coffin is surrounded by the remains of a circular stone structure built for the burial ceremony and covered finally by the earth of the tumulus. Opposite, right: the drawing of a body as it was found.

The deceased of the tumulus grave in Borum Eshoj was stretched out in the coffin, wrapped in his cloak, surrounded by offerings—a box and comb near the head, a sword sheath along the left arm (below). The actual body is on display in the National Museum of Denmark, Copenhagen. The hair was preserved and the box was placed near his head.

wheat, blueberries, and honey. A woman in a tomb at Skrydstrup wore a long skirt made of a woven linen cloth extending down to the feet and attached at the waist. Her ears were adorned with a gold spiral and her hair was drawn in a netting of linen, concealed under a bonnet of the same material.

Deceased men had with them arms of bronze, particularly swords, the attribute of social power. They were dressed in a warm cape covering a tunic secured at the waist. The man of Muldbjerg added to his costume a solid bonnet made of felt. Undergarments consisted of a woven rectangular cloth attached by a belt. Objects of ash, elm, and linden, arranged near the deceased, suggested everyday life: buckets, bowls, cups, spoons, ladles, a folding chair. These individuals with their refined attire lived, as at Vadgard, in large houses grouped together in villages of modest size, dispersed in a rural environment.

Corsica, Sardinia, and the mystery of the "sea peoples"

The fall of Mycenae, around 1200, remains unexplained and has inspired various interpretations. Around 1978

Costume de femme — Age de bronze.
Provenances d'un cercueil de chêne
trouvé au fond du tumulus de
Borum Eshøi près Aarhus
en Jutland, Danmark.

Peigne en corne.

Collier en bronze.

Deux bagues en bronze.

Deux bracelets en bronze.

Cheveu. — la boucle
la plus longue = 0ᵐ75.

Ceinture à houppe
en tissu de laine.

Fibule en

Vase en argile.

Réseau, pourpoint et jupe en tissu
de laine. a-b = 0ᵐ38, b-c = 1ᵐ10
longueur de la ceinture = 2ᵐ52.

Plaque ronde en bronze.

Plaques en bronze.

Poignard en bronze, poignée de corne.

Buried under one of the tumuli of Borum Eshoj, a woman (opposite) was dressed in a short bodice and a skirt. Her head was covered with a bonnet. Among the personal objects of the deceased could be made out, from above, right, a comb, a torque necklace, a ring, a bracelet, a fibula or brooch, a decorative disk worn at the waist, a dagger. A vase must have contained some kind of drink. The man of Trindhoj is from another tumulus of the same community. He was dressed in a tunic extending halfway down his leg and fastened at the waist by a leather thong (left). A cape was thrown over his shoulders as protection against the rigors of winter.

it was attributed by Nancy Sandars to the "sea peoples," as they were also called in the archives of the 19th Dynasty pharaohs. These were peoples who formed a coalition against Egypt, including the "Shardana," depicted wearing horned helmets on the Egyptian bas-relief of Medinet Habu dated precisely to 1190 BC.

Interpreting slightly, we could take the Shardana for Sards and compare the image of the Shardana with that of the statue-menhirs that Roger Grosjean discovered in 1955 at Filitosa in southern Corsica, near the large-scale constructions known as *torri*. In fact, on some of the statues of Corsican warriors—the "Torreans"—the exaggerated head size gives the impression that the head is protected by a helmet, and, in several cases, lateral perforations indicate that horns could be attached. Moreover, the marks on the back of the vertebral column and ribs suggest Shardana bronze breastplates.

Finally, these statue-menhirs fairly often show a chipped carving of a guardman's long sword, evoking Aegean-Mycenaean weapons. The sea peoples must have stopped at Corsica, bearing arms of the same kind used along the European coastlines of the Mediterranean, menacing the Mycenaeans, Phoenicians, and Egyptians at about the same time.

In reality, these statue-menhirs have a long tradition on the island. They must be linked to the megalithic monuments that are so plentiful in Corsica. Corsica and Sardinia are important commercial stopping points, with considerable natural resources, both mineral and vegetal. *Torri* or *nuraghi* appear both as cult structures and as fortified depots, providing shelter for storage. The Corsican Bronze Age, which preserves its own character, shows clear affinities with Sardinia and northern Italy—in particular, the culture and ceramics of the Polada. The influence of southern Italian Apennine culture can be detected also in Sicily and Sardinia. Off the coast of Spain, the Balearic Islands, with their *talayots*

Among the *torri*, or towers, of the site of Filitosa (above), a place of worship and refuge, were erected statue-menhirs with a stylized face and presenting the chipped-out design of a long sword, typical of the tendency to the heroic in the Late Bronze Age.

The *nuraghe,* the equivalent of the Corsican *torre,* gave its name in Sardinia to the civilization known as Nuraghic, which dominated the entire proto-history of the island from the Bronze Age to the Iron Age. The culture maintained contact with Sicily and Italy, as well as with the Balearic Islands and the Iberian Peninsula. At left, the *nuraghe* of Losa, a true fortress.

(tall towers with cyclopean walls that serve as watchtowers in villages of stone huts), similarly demonstrate simultaneously the originality of an island culture as well as the effect of relations with the mainland.

In all these examples long cultural evolutions with increasingly numerous contacts can be seen. The halt of Mycenaean expansion is accompanied by a development of the islands, giving free reign to the growth of local character. Nevertheless, it cannot be viewed as the beginning of a challenge to Greek power.

With its stylized face, long sword, and dagger at the belt, the stela of Filitosa suggests, mistakenly, the "sea peoples." With their stylistic and functional variety (markers of roads and springs, evocation of brave and protective persons), Corsican statue-menhirs, inventoried in 85 monumental sites, are characteristic of the island identity in the Late Bronze Age.

Bronze Age burial rites and other evidence of worship share a number of traits. They seem to reflect a common way of thinking and similar religious or spiritual concepts among the diverse communities residing throughout Europe.

CHAPTER 4

FROM FORCES OF NATURE TO THE BIRTH OF MYTHOLOGY

A tall figure drives a chariot (opposite), with one huge wheel visible, drawn by an ox or bull. The rider, brandishing an ax, is acclaimed by warriors equipped with shields. The scene figures among many chipped carvings in the vast cave site of Tanum, Sweden. At right, a Mycenaean *orant,* a terra-cotta votive figure with raised arms, from Tiryns, 1400–1200 BC, said to be in the shape of the Greek letter phi.

Surviving ancient beliefs: mother goddesses, horned figures

In central and western Europe, the new activity of metallurgy seemed to coincide with a change in worship, even though a certain continuity was also evident. The old agricultural symbols of the Neolithic Age, especially the female deities associated with fertility and the earth, gradually gave way to a more masculine mythology, more consonant with the new reign of minerals and metals. Yet the old-style terra-cotta or bone female figurines continued to be produced and deposited in graves, especially in central Europe and the Balkans. Schematic female amulets of gold, first found in the Varna necropolis in the 5th millennium BC, remained common for a long time.

The old myth of the mother goddess yielded progressively to new concepts. Fire and the sun, as well as their opposite, water, the source of life, were worshiped in central and western Europe. Circles, wheels, spirals, and radiating patterns evoke a certain perpetual dynamism linked to these elements. They were associated with stories of mythological figures and animals, which we can reconstruct from the art of

Placed as burial offerings, these female terra-cotta figurines of the Late Bronze Age (above) come from central Europe. Carvings in the clay simulate jewels, a belt, or embroidered clothing. The arms are placed on the chest and the head is generalized.

The double ax symbolizes the bull's horns. Seen at left is a gold miniature copy, c. 1600 BC, from the offerings in the cave of Arkalochori in Crete.

this period, marked by a great abstraction and a passion for geometry.

Derived from the cult of the bull, which also existed since the Neolithic Age, the celebration of horned symbols appeared in the societies that practiced metallurgy and is found throughout Europe in various forms: pendant motifs, megalithic monument engravings, or themes of rock carvings. In the Aegean they take the form of huge "horns of consecration," frescoes evoking games and combat with the bull, or Cretan or Mycenaean rhytons in the form of a bull's head. In northern Europe these horns decorate anthropomorphic helmets like those from Vikso, Denmark. Deep in a swamp in the Netherlands, researchers in 1957 discovered the "temple" of Bargeroosterveld, with its lintels tapering off at the ends to suggest long horns. This was probably the remains of a sanctuary devoted to the cult of the bull. Inside, small wooden *baetyls* (cult objects for religious display) served to hold offerings. Several bronze hoards were brought to light nearby.

The horned motif appears indirectly and in schematic form in the double axes with rounded blades, suggesting a bull's head. Some thirty copper models were found in north-central Europe, weighing between 1 and 6 pounds (500 grams to 3 kilograms), with a small lateral hole for attaching a handle. These horned models, from the early 2nd millennium, had no funerary associations. They seem related somehow to the votive offerings of miniature double axes of silver or

The rhyton was a drinking vessel in the form of an animal horn or animal head. This example, discovered at Knossos and dated about 1700–1600 BC, was carved from black steatite and has gold-leaf horns. It was intended for libations. The bull's snout has an aperture for pouring.

gold discovered in a rock fissure near Arkalochori, Crete, although no direct link has been discerned. These double axes play an obvious symbolic role in the Cretan-Mycenaean world, since they sometimes are represented between the bull's horns.

Gods engraved in stone open to the sky

The Nordic world is rich in rock carvings, found, for example, in Rogaland and Østfold, Norway; Zealand, Denmark; and Bohuslan and Scania in western and southern Sweden. The boat is the dominant theme. Craft with raised prow suggesting the curved necks of swans or other waterbirds appear emblazoned on rocks by the thousands. Boats in these illustrations sometimes carry warriors brandishing great processional axes, players of *lurer* (large bronze trumpets), or upside-down acrobats. Another frequent theme is the ithyphallic man (with oversized genitalia) pushing a swing plow, in an agricultural scene associated with the cult of fertility and the sun. Bovines, deer species, horses, and animal-drawn war chariots might also be depicted. Some of these iconographic elements—boats, suns, and spirals, in repeating patterns—adorn delicate bronze razors found in the graves of men in these Nordic areas.

A few other European zones, starting in the Neolithic but more commonly since the Chalcolithic and during the Bronze Age, have rock sanctuaries that might cover considerable areas (up to 40 square miles, or 100 square kilometers). The high-altitude sanctuary of Val Camonica, near Brescia, Lombardy, yielded 350,000 engraved drawings (primarily from the Neolithic to the Iron Age); the Valtellina sanctuary, slightly farther north, revealed 25,000; and some 80,000 were found at Mt. Bego, in the Alpes-Maritimes, France. Such carvings

Bronze razors (opposite, below) are found by the hundreds in the Nordic countries. Many feature a finely incised decoration depicting mythological scenes. A boat and spiraling waves, sometimes presented together, are favorite motifs, sometimes associated with birds.

Boats laden with men, some standing and others kneeling with one arm raised, as depicted in some small Nordic bronzes of the Late Bronze Age, were engraved on a flagstone some 35 feet (10 meters) long, found at Tanum, Sweden (left). At the prow and stern, the boats bear schematized figures, such as a horse's head, an elk, or a bird. At the center of the panel a man who seems to be the principal figure in the scene is perched on a chariot (represented by a wheel) drawn by a bull (shown on page 84). Boats are a recurring theme in Nordic cave art. Gathered in large groups in some compositions, they can evoke a heroic episode in the history of a people or a great mythical journey.

portray the emblematic animals; the bull predominates at Mt. Bego, the deer in Val Camonica, the elk in Scandinavia. The routes marked off by rock carvings may have commemorated mythical journeys.

Water, source of life

Cult sites and structures give evidence of the veneration of water in the Bronze Age. One such structure could be found at the thermal spring at St.-Moritz in Switzerland, at

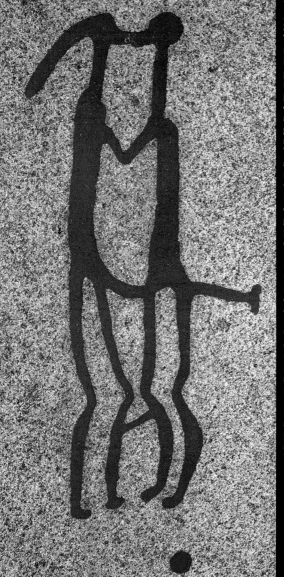

In the Bohuslän region of southwestern Sweden (particularly at Tanum), some 120,000 rock figures have been inventoried. They were produced by chipping the rock with the help of a punching instrument (of quartzite, for instance) and by adding a color generally lighter than the shade of the rock surface. The passage of sunlight across the surface sufficed to enliven these figures. It was not unusual, starting in the Bronze Age, for an ocher paint to be used for greater contrast. The present coloring, which clearly defines the shapes, is a modern addition. In the panel at left, the figures most likely are hunters armed with ax or bow, associated with deer. The same scene is depicted at Val Camonica, Italy, also chipped into the rock. In the center, bent figures hold a club in one hand as they apparently perform a dance. A boat is seen below, and the four animals at the top are perhaps elk. The panel on the right shows a couple embracing.

an altitude of some 6,000 feet (1,800 meters). Still in use in the 19th century, it was associated with offerings that dated back to the 12th century BC.

Similarly, ceremonial hoards of wind instruments—Danish bronze *lurer*, left in pairs, or Irish horns, also of bronze—associated with treasures of jewelry and gold dishes, have been found in swamps.

Usually played in pairs, large bronze *lurer,* trumpet-type instruments made of several molded pieces fitted together which produce a deep sound, are reminiscent of the two horns of a bull. Left: a Danish *lur.*

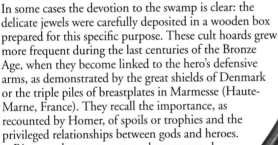

In some cases the devotion to the swamp is clear: the delicate jewels were carefully deposited in a wooden box prepared for this specific purpose. These cult hoards grew more frequent during the last centuries of the Bronze Age, when they become linked to the hero's defensive arms, as demonstrated by the great shields of Denmark or the triple piles of breastplates in Marmesse (Haute-Marne, France). They recall the importance, as recounted by Homer, of spoils or trophies and the privileged relationships between gods and heroes.

Rivers and streams were no less venerated than springs and swamps. This is confirmed by numerous bronze objects—especially weapons—thrown into these waters from the Early to the Late Bronze Age, particularly in the latter. A great number of swords and spearheads, along with a few helmets, were submerged in the mouth of the Loire, in

Excavations in the springs of St.-Moritz revealed offerings and working equipment from the Bronze Age (sketches above): a larch framework containing two wells that drew groundwater.

This wide bronze neck piece from Loshult, Sweden, 1500–500 BC, formed part of a woman's ensemble. It is decorated with three rows of continuous spirals, a typical ornamental motif of Nordic Bronze Age cultures that is also found as far away as the Aegean basin.

Nine bronze breastplates (below), packed inside one another in sets of three, were found in Marmesse (Haute-Marne, France). This ceremonial armor, from 9th–8th century BC, probably highly polished, may have formed an offering.

the Seine, the Garonne, the Rhône, the Saône, the Rhine, and many other European rivers. Most were thrown in intact, but some had been damaged by fire. In certain spots along riverbanks or near the shores of lakes, an extraordinary concentration of armor as well as pottery or organic remains can be interpreted as the traces of shoreline sanctuaries, unless these were trading posts, frontier territories or border crossing areas, or fords, where offerings may have been accumulated.

Small bronze figures as individual offerings

Several cultural groups produced small bronze statuettes, the most famous of which were the Sardinian *bronzetti*. Such statuettes might have been offerings at springs or placed in sacred wells or in sectors of *nuraghi* reserved for worship. Production of such pieces began in the Late

Bronze Age and reached its peak between 900 and 500 BC, which means it continued into the Iron Age. The same can be said of the small Greek, Etruscan, and Iberian bronzes, all of which lasted even longer. This type of object, however, is not exclusively Mediterranean. Produced in lesser numbers, the small Nordic bronzes also reflect Late Bronze Age society. Thus, two kneeling warriors wearing horned helmets from Grevensvaenge, Denmark, have a model in Vikso. As certain carvings

The theme of the acrobat was treated both in the Nordic countries (opposite, below: a figurine from Zealand, Denmark, 600 BC) and in the Aegean world. The small female figures from Pomerania and Scania, on the southern and northern shores of the Baltic (left), are depicted nude, adorned with a twisted torque necklace.

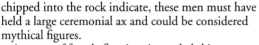

Small Sardinian bronzes portray warriors, shepherds, praying figures, and women, as well as votive boats, birds, musicians, and other figures, giving expression to the Nuraghic civilization, which arose in the Bronze Age. Opposite, above: a warrior wears a helmet with round-tipped horns. The double shield he carries can be compared to the "figure-of-eight" Mycenaean shield, carried vertically, which covered the entire body.

chipped into the rock indicate, these men must have held a large ceremonial ax and could be considered mythical figures.

A group of female figurines in corded skirts, one leaning over backward in an acrobat's posture along with some others standing, in long skirts, seemed to form part of an organized scene that included the helmeted males. Some of these small female statuettes decorate knife handles or brooches.

Race to the sun: horses, chariots, wheels, and birds

The sun and solar cults assume great importance during the Bronze Age. They are linked to fire—so important for metallurgy—to the universe, and also to journeys, which demand new geographical and astronomical knowledge.

In western Europe these cults left archaeological evidence that bears some relationship to the myth of Apollo's seasonal journey on a chariot drawn by swans, transmitted by ancient authors. Gold disks, miniature chariots, birds, and horses pertain to this new mythological climate.

Bronze wheels with four spokes, dating to the Early Bronze Age in Ardalia, Transylvania, and in Obisovce, Slovakia, were buried in pairs unrelated to any archaeological context. The large bronze wheels of the type seen at Coulon, in Charente, France, represent metallurgical triumphs: they were apparently cast in a single piece. The number of buried wheels varies: one at Coulon; two at Le Fa, in the Aude, and in Hassloch, southwestern Germany, the latter deliberately broken into 193 fragments; four at Stade, not far away. The hoards of harnessing equipment, common between the Elbe and Vistula Rivers, likewise make reference to horses, and they also seem to have an unusual association with feminine ornamentation. The cult of the horse, which was domesticated at the same period, is linked to the Bronze Age. The head and mane of a horse decorate the gold cups of the Danish treasure of Borgbjerg. But the most representative object of this mythology is undoubtedly the votive wagon from Trundholm, in northern Zealand, Denmark, discovered in 1902 in a former swamp. The piece is one of a kind: only one other wagon has reportedly been found, in 1895, at Hälsingborg, Sweden, composed of two small horses and a disk, but it has disappeared. The famous terra-cotta chariot of Dupljaja, Serbia, on the other hand, is drawn by three waterbirds. These motifs may replace one another; some ceramic vases consist of birds' bodies surmounted by a bull's head, and the like. The association of the waterbird with solar symbols is typical of religious expression in the Bronze Age. Birds, like horses, are connected with the sun, as is particularly evident in northern Europe. The link appears as well in the Cretan and Mycenaean world, for instance, on the sarcophagus of Hagia Triada, Crete, decorated with a painted procession showing many symbolic objects, including double axes crowned with birds.

Vases mounted on four small wheels may refer to such divine vehicles. These are urns containing the incinerated remains of important individuals of the Late Bronze Age. Their tombs generally include rich grave furnishings. The use of vessels on wheels continues with some variations to the end of the Bronze Age and the beginning of the Iron Age; these burials are undoubtedly the source of the great chariot tombs that occur later.

The miniature terra-cotta chariot found at Dupljaja, Serbia, dated from the Middle Bronze Age (opposite, above), is decorated with bird's heads. The mobile statuette depicts a male figure wearing a robe decorated with solar motifs (circles impressed in the clay), also adorned with a bird's head, like certain Aegean idols. He probably carried a parasol.

The Trundholm sun wagon served as a toy for a farmer's daughter before it was identified by archaeologists. While it was partly broken by the farmer's plow, other older damage, on the other hand, indicates that it had been voluntarily sacrificed before it was abandoned. It is composed of two parts: a bronze disk plated with gold leaf (preserved on one side) decorated with circular motifs based on the spiral, and a bronze horse with carvings that simulate a mane and a harness. Both are fixed to a platform constituting a wagon on six wheels.

A solar sanctuary

Stonehenge, the most famous of the megalithic monuments, is not a construction for funerary use, at least not as arranged in the Bronze Age, but is considered an astronomical temple. According to excavations carried out in the past century on the site, four phases of construction can be distinguished. Its original construction was begun at the end of the Neolithic and completed in the Bronze Age. This period saw the building of the monumental structures, such as the outer sarsen circle (sandstone uprights with their lintels), the outer circle of bluestones, the inner horseshoe of trilithons, and so on. The principal axis, which cuts through the middle of the circle and the Heel Stone—a small orientation stone arranged 100 feet (30 meters) from the outer bank at the northeast—meets up on the horizon with the precise spot where the sun appears on the day of the summer solstice, whose determination made it possible to establish the agricultural calendar. Astrophysicist Gerald Hawkins carried astronomical theories further and conjectured that the fifty-six peripheral postholes and the thirty raised stones in the central area were intended to link the solar system to the lunar system, which is more complex, and in particular to predict eclipses.

Stonehenge, in southern England—one of the greatest European sites linked to the cult of the sun—testifies to the birth of the science of astronomy. In the Bronze Age it reached its full, monumental size, before 1500 BC. The central portion has an outer circle of sarsen (sandstone) uprights and lintels, inside which lies a circle of smaller bluestones and and an inner horseshoe of higher stones.

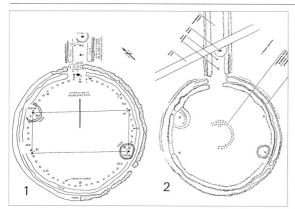

The triumph of gold

Gold, the luminous metal of enduring brightness, like amber was a prized material in the Bronze Age, extracted profusely from various European deposits and produced in record quantities.

In treasures dedicated to the gods of nature, gold-smithing imparted its most important message. This raw material, fashioned into heavy jewelry or flamboyant vessels, became a collective, deliberate gift bestowed on

The sketch at left (1) represents the first two phases of construction of Stonehenge: the circular ditch, the 56 so-called Aubrey Holes (thought to be postholes), and the entry of the so-called Avenue with the Heel Stone (an orientation stone, above). The sketch at right (2) shows the incomplete circle of bluestones in the center. Through its different phases, it worked the same way: on the day of the summer solstice, an observer situated in the center of the monument looks northeast to the Heel Stone, which indicates the rising sun on the horizon. This stone is placed in the axis of a ceremonial avenue.

forces of nature: water, trees, mountains. These ritual offerings, which can seem irrational today, are central to the western Bronze Age. In contrast, gold in the Mycenaean world is associated at an early stage with the glorification of dead heroes. Later, beginning with the Iron Age, the use of gold would be subjected increasingly to "political" power, and as trade developed, the offering to the gods would give way to currency.

In the beginning of the 2nd millennium, the extreme western parts of Europe produced a series of fine necklaces of beaten gold that took the form of crescents decorated with incised geometric shapes. Called lunulae, they are among the oldest gold treasures found in this region. Later, in the

The cone of Avanton (Vienne, France), at left, was discovered in 1844. Like the three other gold cones discovered to date, its function remains a mystery. Is it a hat? a vessel? Only the one in Schifferstadt (Rhineland-Palatinate, Germany) was accompanied by furnishings—palstaves—which date it to the end of the Middle Bronze Age. The circles and other motifs punched on these tall gold-leaf cones must have been obtained by applying matrices against the external surface of these great objects, a painstaking and laborious process of stamping and trimming.

Middle and Late Bronze Age, heavy, massive necklaces or smooth bracelets constituted typical offerings of the western peoples. Some gold necklaces weighed more than 4 pounds (2 kilograms). The same period saw the production of cups and goblets of beaten gold, decorated with stamped circles depicting the sun. These goblets were buried, sometimes with jewels or bronze vessels, and seem to be the remains of ceremonial services. On the other hand, mystery still surrounds the use of four great gold cones, three of them from a region between northern Switzerland and the southern Rhineland of Germany, the fourth from west-central France. They measure between 24 and 36 inches (60 to 90 centimeters) high and represent technical feats of goldsmithing.

Aegean nature worship...

In the Aegean world the finest preserved remains date from 1600 to 1400 BC, a period marked by open-air sanctuaries, religious buildings, and objects or representations of religious ceremonies, about which very little is known. On the other hand, the documents in Linear B at Pylos, Mycenae, and Knossos supply a few clues, such as the names of certain deities,

Gold was rarely used for dishes. Most gold vessels are concentrated in northern and central Europe and in the Aegean. In the north they are most often found in hoards of offerings, decorated with rectilinear patterns, chevrons, or circles; Aegean examples, decorated with spirals, come from tombs. Above, a Nordic vase from the Late Bronze Age, decorated with rows of zigzags and chevrons. The lower part of the vase presents a starred motif. Left: common types of gold bracelets from central Europe, from the Middle Bronze Age: bars hammered and rolled into cylinders and a massive piece decorated with grooves, forming a kind of cuff.

information on their ceremonies, and gifts that were offered to them.

The Mycenaeans shared many beliefs with the Minoans, yet nowhere on the mainland of Greece do we find remains of "lustral basins" (for purification rituals), "horns of consecration," stone "libation tables," and sanctuaries located on a high point (known as peak sanctuaries) that form a good part of the Minoan cult apparatus. Minoan religion produced sanctuaries in each village, which filled with votive offerings over the course of several generations. These were open-air sanctuaries, with flat or raised altars, sometimes at the top of staircases, ornamented with sacred horns, double axes, tripods, trees, or branches. In these sacred places people placed crowns, libation vases, rhytons, bronze and terra-cotta figurines in human or animal form (birds, insects), amulets, and seal rings. Many sanctuaries occupied natural sites. At Knossos, the cave of Eileithyia near Amnisos preserved offerings left in place since the Late

Minoan civilization has left extensive records of an intense religious life. On a painted terra-cotta sarcophagus from Hagia Triada (Crete), 15th century BC, a procession bearing offerings comes before the deity, who stands under a tree and behind an altar in an outdoor sanctuary. The offerings are calves and a miniature boat, perhaps of precious metal (similar to a silver model found in Naxos).

Neolithic, and tablets indicate offerings of honey and linen clothing. In the cave of Nirou Khani, gigantic double axes and more than forty altars on tripod had been deposited. At Gournia, in the town center, a small sanctuary contains cult objects: cylinders and snake idols.

The cave of Arkalochori, a mountain sanctuary, contains warrior offerings, especially the famous double axes in gold associated with long swords. The seal rings, of gold or precious stone, present miniature depictions of cult groupings in the open air where the deity seems to interact with both women and men. These sanctuaries sheltered ritual dances, processions, ceremonies enacted by the faithful in front of altars or trees. Other themes found here include the seated goddess, probably originating from the mainland, who is also encountered on stelae and paintings, a theme that continued to the Classical era.

Constructed sanctuaries are very rare. At Khania in a small quadrangular building with a stone floor, six rooms were devoted to worship. This site contained numerous terra-cotta votive figurines portraying the snake goddess, dated about 1300 BC. The Temple of Karphi is a small sanctuary with five goddesses of terra-cotta, an altar, and a three-wheeled chariot. Decorated with bull's heads, this chariot is drawn by a man.

On the Greek mainland in the Mycenaean

The snake goddess, of faience or glazed terra-cotta, from Knossos (1700–1600 BC) provides information on female clothing of the day. Her costume—a flounced skirt, a bodice tightened around the waist and leaving the breasts bare— is copied in Minoan frescoes. The bird on her head and the snake in each hand are the attributes that recall the heavenly and infernal elements of Cretan religion.

era, the mode of expression changed. The great goddess takes a variety of forms—bird, snake, mountain, tree, wind, and sea; she also appears as the war goddess. The sacred horn motif continues to be associated with architecture. A new accessory of the female costume appears: a knot, worn in back, shown in faience decorative works that may also have been offerings. Vase decorations—on great vases mounted on chariots or for cult use, like rhytons—repeat the theme of the chariot procession, of the goddess receiving demons, or of altars, often portable, decorated with vegetation and sacred horns and, between them, the double ax.

Frescoes offer invaluable evidence of religious customs. They show the theme of sacred horns, of the knot (which adorns the back of "La Parisienne" at Knossos). The sacred role of the woman appears at Thera, Tiryns, Mycenae, Pylos, where "priestesses" parade in a procession bearing votive vases.

...and the emergence of a first pantheon

At Knossos, the "priestess of the winds" officiated. At Pylos on the mainland, male gods as well as female are recorded as receiving the offerings—honey, coriander, oil, linen, cheese, wine, sheep, gold vases, spices, and so on—listed in tablets written in Linear B. In this way they introduce a new pantheon, including, alongside Atana, the goddess of horses, Poseidon, the most revered, then Zeus, associated with Hera, as well as Hermes, Ares, Erinys, Dionysus, Potnia. Those not mentioned include

During processions or cult ceremonies before the deity, the faithful held rhytons of a type resembling this terra-cotta model, from Akrotiri, c. 1600 BC, decorated with rows of spiral motifs. The conic shape and decoration contributed to a confusion between such a vessel and the gold cones of central Europe.

Apollo, Hephaestus, Aphrodite, and Demeter. Minor deities, such as the pigeon goddess, enjoyed the same kind of offerings: gold cups, animals such as bulls, cows, pigs, sheep. The calendar of festivals shows that priests and priestesses had precise attributes and were sometimes attached to a particular god. It is often difficult to know whether the individuals mentioned in the lists were intended for the service of the gods or designated as victims of sacrifice. Officials busied themselves organizing the collective ceremonies and saw to the procurement of the goods necessary for banquets (livestock, olives, wine). Texts from Pylos indicate that one initiation festival reportedly involved more than a thousand worshipers.

Sanctuaries in Mycenaean Greece, often hard to distinguish from regular houses, take the form of a series of rooms set around a courtyard. The room reserved for worship was generally elongated, equipped with a bench on which sacred statuettes were arranged. In the palace, the *megaron* (principal hall), with its central foyer and its mural decorations, may have served as place of worship. Apparently, two levels could be distinguished in Mycenaean religion: a popular faith, as indicated primarily by the terra-cotta figurines, and an official religion organized in the palaces by a rigorous administration that kept accounts of the offerings.

According to a few tablets, deities possessed property: Potnia, for example, owned flocks at Knossos, blacksmiths at Pylos, as well as slaves. Archaeological evidence demonstrates that workshops producing the offerings were

The famous "Parisienne" of Knossos was no doubt taking part in a procession. This is the only surviving fragment of the fresco in which she figures; it presents her in profile. She owes her nickname and her popularity to the expression of radiant youth and elegance, which, on her discovery at the turn of the century, suggested the proverbial chic of the women of Paris. She wears on her back a mysterious "knot," a sacred Minoan symbol.

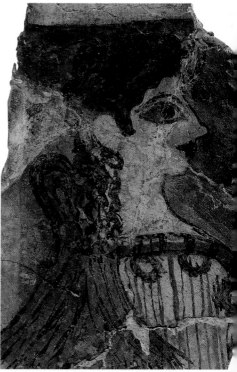

Left: two seal stone imprints, the first showing a cult scene. A warrior, spear in hand, stands before vases and a sword, which may be his offerings. The tree he faces certainly suggests an open-air sanctuary. At right, a woman, probably a deity, is shown dressed in the characteristic Cretan flounced skirt.

located next to the sanctuaries; this was the case at Mycenae for ivory work, metallurgy, and objects in faience.

Gods and rites cited by Homer

Finally, in the *Odyssey* and above all in the *Iliad,* Homer referred to the religion of the period, the bonds between gods and humans, and the places sacred to cults. He described temples, altars, and offerings. Some of the gods he mentions were already cited on the tablets written in Linear B.

Among the rites he evokes, Homer makes recurring references to libations, which meant pouring wine on the ground, and animal sacrifices. The latter came relatively late; remains of burned animal bones do not appear before the end of the Bronze Age or the beginning of the Iron Age. Offerings are specific to each god. Thus, Nestor sacrifices to Athena a calf and a heifer after having their horns gilded, while a five-year-old bull is sacrificed to Zeus and offerings made of a libation of wine, a steer's plump thigh, a ram, a boar, and so on.

A gold seal ring from Tiryns, 15th century BC. The carving shows half-human, half-animal beings bearing libation vases and facing the great goddess, who holds a large conical vase.

Homer also describes the worship of springs: Odysseus and Eumaois pass "a spring house where the people filled their jars.... Ice cold in runnels from a high rock ran the spring, and over it there stood an altar stone to the cool nymphs, where all men going by laid offerings" (*Odyssey*, 17:212–19).

The links between religion and nature are omnipresent in all parts of Europe in the Bronze Age. A homogeneity of beliefs and cults makes itself felt through several common elements: natural sanctuaries, the attraction of springs, the mythic role of the bull, of birds, and of chariots. Certain particularities stand out nevertheless, notably, a clearly more abstract mode of expression in the non-Mediterranean cultures, the great metallurgists, while statuettes and depictions of female deities are more persistent in the Aegean world, which is perhaps more traditional.

The ivory group known as "Demeter, Kora, and the divine child" was found in the sanctuary of the Palace of Mycenae (15th century BC). Demeter, goddess of earth fertility, periodically regained her daughter Persephone, also known as Kora, who had been carried off to Hades. The scene depicted here remains mysterious, and the name applied to it owes more to poetry than to scientific rigor. Nevertheless, sculpted with precision, it reveals details of female clothing: bodice, wide flounced skirt, bracelets, and neck-laces. Ivories did not truly appear until the second palace period in Crete and the rise of Mycenaean power. These figurines were probably exchanged as prestige gifts.

After the fall of Mycenae (about 1100 BC), Greece entered a so-called dark age, about which little is known. The other parts of Europe, meanwhile, were flourishing. The end of the period was marked everywhere by abrupt change and the adoption of a new metal—iron—which ended the Bronze Age.

CHAPTER 5
THE HIGH BRONZE AGE: A TIME OF UPHEAVAL?

The Late Bronze Age is the "age of warriors," who are everywhere depicted in heroic guise. In Spain the Iberian stela of Solana de Cabañas (opposite) shows a combatant with his attributes (weapons, jewelry, chariot). A small ivory head from Mycenae (right) wears a boar's-tusk helmet described by Homer.

The last period of the Bronze Age shows a certain continuity with that preceding it. It reveals societies in full flower that mastered the manufacture of bronze, which spread progressively and was used for domestic implements. At the same time, between 1200 and 800 BC, cremation became more common, replacing inhumation burial in funeral rites, and it came to typify the final phase of the Bronze Age and the beginning of the Iron Age, depending on the regions involved, and signaled an initial rupture. Meanwhile, the abundance of metal weapons, attested everywhere, confirms the increased importance of military uses of metallurgy and indicates a time of turbulence. More attentive observation of the remains in their context allows us, first, to define the dynamic groups and to understand more clearly the different types of upheaval.

The "high Bronze Age" of the Swiss lake villages and its sudden disappearance about 850 BC

The "high Bronze Age" was defined by Edouard Desor, in 1865, on the basis of numerous remains of the lake settlements of the Lake of Neuchâtel. Recent excavations caused by the construction of an expressway in this

Lakeside settlements, sometimes called lake villages, appeared in the Neolithic Age in Alpine regions and more sporadically in the Bronze Age. The reconstruction sketch of the site of Cortaillod-Est on the Lake of Neuchâtel, Switzerland (below), shows how the village was organized to take advantage of both its rural mountain location and the lake environment, which favored fishing and trade.

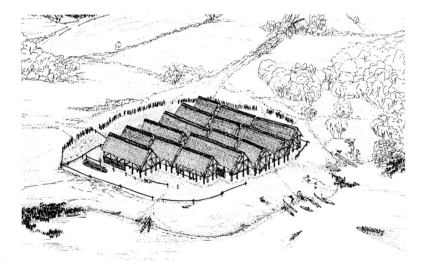

region give a precise idea of the activity and the chronology of entire villages, like Hauterive-Champréveyres, inhabited between 1040 and 870 BC (according to dendrochronological studies, or dating by means of growth rings in trees) over an area of 21 acres (8.5 hectares). Two dynamic construction phases were determined and a total of 7,500 poles identified, proving that the three large houses of the first phase, and then the others, possessed a floor raised some 6½ feet (2 meters) above ground, which was seasonally flooded. The village of Auvernier on the banks of the same Lake of Neuchâtel, or Mörigen on the shore of the Lake of Biel (Lac du Bienne), or the settlements around Lake Bourget (Savoie, France) accumulated thousands of bronze objects, including axes with deep flanges; swords; daggers; spearheads and arrowheads; knives; fishhooks; a great variety of pins, plaques, rings, wheels, horse-harness ornaments; amber and glass beads; lignite bracelets. The agricultural way of life seemed prosperous. Botanical study of the organic remains has shown that wheat, barley, and many vegetables were cultivated and established which species were used for the manufacture of one tool or another. The Alps furnished copper ore and the resources for a migratory way of life that exploited increasing areas of alpine land. Contacts were proven with northern Italy, with central Europe, and, more rarely, with the Atlantic zone.

How can we account for the sudden, definitive desertion of the lake settlements in the mid-11th century BC? A natural catastrophe such as exceptional rains may have submerged most of the sites north of the Alps. Rather precise dates, obtained by means of dendrochronology, agree from one site to another but do not help us to understand the fate of the residents of these lakeside villages and why they left these areas.

Along the shore of Lake Bourget (Savoie, France), remains of the "high Bronze Age" are plentiful. Among terra-cotta objects found there, a ring-shaped object (above, left) can be interpreted as a stand for a narrow-based vase decorated with tin strips (to the right of the ring). Above, right, is one of two parts of a sandstone mold that served to cast bronze rings. The metallic objects are ornamental plaques, razors, bracelets, a spearhead, knife blades, and a scythe. They were discovered underwater; the bronze retained its original yellow tint.

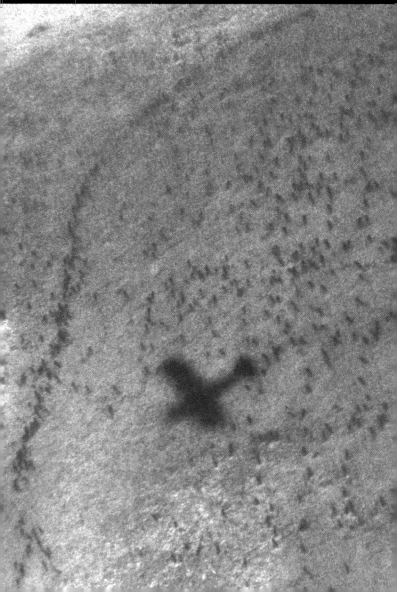

Following the spectacular lowering of the waters of Swiss lakes caused by the regulatory plan adopted in the 19th century, many stakes or piles appeared, revealing the structure of the "lake villages." Aerial photographs, as seen here in Champréveyres on the Lake of Neuchâtel, reveal rows of piles outlining the rectangular plan of houses. These piles supported platforms that served as a floor for the dwellings. Recent research proves that these towns were definitely built in sites subject to flooding, though not directly on the lakes themselves.

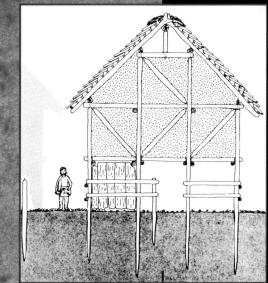

Fortified camps and warriors of central Europe

Among the great fortified sites, Velim–St. Veit, Hungary, on a promontory defended by ramparts and ditches, brought together farmers and craftsmen—potters, metallurgists, and weavers, whose raw materials came from the south, that is, the neighboring Alps, and from the north, as in the case of amber beads. This type of centralized organization seems to foreshadow what Caesar in the Iron Age called the *oppidum*, the original equivalent of the social and legal reality that was the Mediterranean city. The retrenching was more than symbolic, as is proven by the weapons found in great number during excavations early in the 20th century and in 1973, including arrowheads of bronze and especially flint, spearheads, and a few sword blades.

Swords with metal hilt, then tanged, were particularly, and proportionally, numerous in the beds of rivers such as the Rhine or the Danube, where they had been thrown as offerings. Though burned and broken, they continued to symbolize the male presence in the remains of ashes left in ceramic urns with a lid and placed, with one or more vases of offerings, in the cemeteries known as urnfields.

The phenomenon of the urnfields

From the Lausitzer Neisse River at the border of eastern Germany and Poland, thought to be the source of these funerary ceramics, to Catalonia, where similar vases were found, three principal phases have been interpreted as the result of three invasions (the fourth introduced iron).

The typical warrior or supposed invader was reconstructed on the basis of finds scattered in the hoards of offerings, with bronze weapons, a crested helmet, a breastplate of the style of Fillinges (Savoie, France), a shield, greaves, and a sword. Many hoards also contained debris of a vessel, or *situla*, no doubt intended to hold an alcoholic drink, served during the cremation ceremony. This *situla*, accompanied by a handled cup, like the defensive armor

The funerary urn, of ceramic (opposite, various models from a cemetery in Romania shown in cross section to reveal the interior of the urn with the ashes of the departed) or bronze (below, from Germany, 9th–8th century BC) was covered with a flat top or lid. Offerings were arranged inside or, after the urn was placed in a filled-in ditch, set on top of the lid.

The image of the hero idealized in death, accompanied by his weapons and ornaments, appears on some Iberian stelae. Archaeologists have reconstructed the typical armaments of a warrior of the final period of the Bronze Age (below), but these efforts have yet to be confirmed by the discovery of an entire set of equipment within a single site.

was in bronze sheet, decorated in repoussé with small juxtaposed bosses outlining solar and bird-shaped motifs.

The change of funerary rite has been explained as due to historic events: "Urnfield peoples," from Lusatia, were believed to have spread out in waves toward the south and the west. Once arrived in southeastern Europe, these people, it was believed, called themselves Dorians.

Close examination of their articles of bronze and ceramics, their decorative styles, and their production techniques reveals strong local identities, suggesting durable settlements that contradict the hypothesis of massive, rapid invasions. The diffusion of certain prestige objects, which seems to confirm the notion of migrations, was actually the result of highly developed craftsmanship, trade, and diplomacy.

The peak of the Atlantic Bronze Age

Vases decorated in the style of the funerary ceramics of the Rhine area and Switzerland also appeared farther west in fortified sites in the Neolithic tradition such as at Fort-Harrouard, in the district of Sorel-Moussel (Eure-et-Loir, France). In an area covering 17 acres (7 hectares), protected by ramparts and a moat, Late Bronze Age houses surround a large central space. The site yielded evidence of richly varied artisans' activity, including about one hundred bronze workers' molds, of which more than half proved to be for weapons, the greatest number being spearheads, followed by swords, arrowheads, and finally daggers. Since these proportions do not match those of the actual weapons found at the site, we can conclude that these foundries produced spears and swords that were dispersed throughout the region.

The system of symbolism borne by the arms and also by the jewelry further suggests a firm identity and a strong power, while the great number and variety of products convey the impression of a dynamic period.

Left: this woman's ornament made from a boar tusk encased in a bronze-wire setting was found in the tomb of La Colombine in Champlay (Yonne, France). Opposite: a bronze warrior's helmet discovered at Blainville (Moselle, France).

The fortified site of Fort-Harrouard at Sorel-Moussel (Eure-et-Loir, France) occupies a plateau between a dry valley and the valley of the Eure. The ramparts that went across the hill are believed to have been located in the foreground to the right. A major craft center, particularly for metallurgy, the community was not self-sufficient. The surrounding region provided its raw materials (wood, charcoal, clay, stones) and agricultural products (grains and domestic animals). The abundant local fauna (deer and boars) was also exploited. The fortification protected the fragile equilibrium of this system.

Examples include hundreds of vases found in the cave of Rancogne (Charente, France), the dozens of bronzes and, especially, weapons thrown into rivers—the Meuse, Thames, Seine, Loire, Dordogne—as well as thousands of broken articles stored in the "hoards."

Intensive stockpiling of bronze objects: hoarding for a crisis?

The hoard at Vénat (Charente, France), placed in a cylindrical vase and hidden in a ditch, contained more than three thousand fragments of bronze objects—weapons, jewelry, tools—mostly from the Atlantic zone, but also from southern and central European workshops. Were these pieces intended for recasting? Or could they be cult offerings? The discarding of metal objects was a familiar phenomenon since the Early Bronze Age, but the increasing deposits of debris in the Late Bronze Age has also been taken as the concealment of wealth, the sign of a troubled period.

On the basis of these hoards, we can refine the chronology and the characteristics of the period. In France, the "Tréboul hoard" phase, characterized by palstaves dating to the end of the Middle Bronze Age, is followed in the Late Bronze Age by the Rosnoen phase, with bipartite-tanged swords, then the St.-Brieuc-des-Iffs phase, with tripartite-tanged swords, and finally the Vénat phase, with carp's-tongue swords.

In Britain the same kind of evolution can be seen, with the successive hoards of the type from Penard, then Wilburton, and finally Ewart Park. The 50-foot (15-meter) boat found at Dover in 1992 suggests trade beyond the English Channel and along the Atlantic coasts, in a range

The urn from the cave of Rancogne (Charente, France) was hidden along with metallic and organic offerings in a place reserved for the dead. The retreat of populations into caves and the choice of these hidden spots for funerary customs like the hoarding of bronze articles convey a general impression of insecurity.

of products such as bronzes
of the kind found in the
water of Langdon Bay, near
Dover, or at Huelva, Spain.

A new metal for
a new civilization

After the fall of Mycenae—
though not necessarily
caused by it—a series of
destructions created a
situation favorable to the
introduction of a new metal,
iron, which would gradually
replace bronze and transform
the entire society. Transition to the Iron Age was
assuredly not due entirely to advances in metallurgy,
which yielded a strong, flexible iron that quickly
became effective and inexpensive. Whereas bronze
spears and swords were swiftly replaced by iron
weapons, as is seen in the "ceramic
cemetery" of Athens, for example, the
new metal was adopted more slowly
in the Ebro valley, where it
was used for fibulae or
brooches. However, within
two or three centuries, iron
dominated weaponry and
jewelry production, leaving
bronze as the material for
priestly vessels and a few
items of jewelry such as
bracelets.

The Bronze Age in
the formation of a
European culture

The Bronze Age truly
existed in Europe.
Reservations voiced by certain
archaeologists remain

At the end of the
Bronze Age, between
900 and 800 BC, many
hoards were set up in circular ditches (above, a
hoard of socketed axes at
Plestin-les-Grèves, Côtes-
d'Armor, France). Most
objects recovered from
these sites were composed
of alloys rich in lead and
thus extremely malleable;
however, they had not
been used in ways sug-
gested by their forms.
Rather, they were
considered premonetary
currency. As many as one
thousand can be found
at one time. Hidden
along paths or in swampy
sites, perhaps sacred in
nature, they may have
been offerings.

The hoard at Larnaud
(Jura, France) yielded
hundreds of bronze
objects (left), perhaps
collected for recasting.

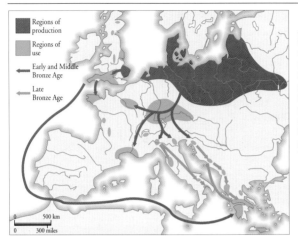

Regions of
production

Regions of
use

← Early and Middle
Bronze Age

← Late
Bronze Age

0   500 km
0   300 miles

Amber, used particularly to make beads, came from deposits situated along the Baltic and in eastern England. The routes amber presumably followed in its dispersal in the Bronze Age formed a series of linkages between northern and southern Europe.

unfounded. Neolithic agricultural-pastoral society was relegated to the countryside with its megalithic monuments and its villages, making the fortified sites and palaces the centers of a new power where commerce and craftsmanship developed. The work in copper and other metals was the source of new wealth. Horizons expanded; trade in raw materials and the export of craft techniques and objects linked Egypt, Phoenicia, Cyprus, Crete, and mainland Greece, which sent its products throughout the Mediterranean beginning in the Minoan period. In the north, trade undoubtedly did not follow the model of Greek colonization. However, there is ample evidence to suggest that a relatively homogeneous cultural entity had grown up from north to south and from east to west, not only through trade in Baltic amber, in cassiterite, a tin oxide indispensable for making bronze—exported from Cornwall in Great Britain—and in bronze vessels, but also through the diffusion of the same decorative motifs, such as the waterbird. Many other kinds of objects—swords, spearheads, horned helmets, shields, breastplates, pins, brooches, and bracelets—were widely diffused throughout Europe. Similarly, the engraved or repoussé solar decorations testify to shared traditions. Votive chariots, Greek and Iberian stelae, Alpine and Scandinavian rock carvings confirm the common beliefs that give the impression of a true civilization. That the comparison of texts could shed light on this civilization explains why the issue of dating Homer's narrative remains central to scientific debate.

The Trojan War: a historic event?

Homeric legend reports that East and West confronted one another for many years along the Anatolian coast, at Troy, until the city was destroyed. Behind these Greek and Anatolian actors, two worlds clashed. The legend reveals for the first time the historic consciousness of the Greeks and of their destiny in the formation of Europe.

First of all was the historic event. According to the Hittite archives found at Boghazköy, the conquest and sacking of Troy may have been one of the incidents of the expedition launched by the "Ahhiyawā," believed to be the Achaeans, against the north coast of Anatolia between the beginning of the 14th and the end of the 13th century BC. In the epic narrative, the poet (not held to accuracy) gave this event an exaggerated scope, surely disproportionate to reality.

The wagon bearing a cauldron from Orastia (Romania, 9th–8th century BC) is a cult object left as a funerary offering (above). It is adorned with twelve heads of waterbirds (six on each side), a common iconographic theme throughout Europe, found in central Europe and the Nordic region as well. The repoussé bronze urn from Vulci, Italy (left), decorated with stylized bird motifs, is from the same period.

Secondly, there is archaeological evidence. In Troy VI and VIIa, experts have uncovered abundant Mycenaean remains, which demonstrate a Greek presence and lend credence to the Homeric narrative of the fall of Troy and its ensuing destruction.

For a century, experts have debated whether the Homeric text informs us only about the period when the poems took shape, formalized about 700 BC, or if linguistic study would reveal traces of an earlier period, specifically that of the Trojan War and the Bronze Age.

A historian's reticence

In 1956 the publication of Moses Finley's *The World of Odysseus* revived the issue, at a time when many researchers believed that the *Iliad* not only related events of the Bronze Age but also described the society of the great palaces of Mycenae and Pylos, as well as the fortress of Troy, exhumed by the discoveries of Schliemann, Blegen, and others. Linear B was just being deciphered, which made it clear that Homer's text, composed around 700 BC in a new alphabetical language, was later than the Mycenaean tablets. The question was whether the described events were also later. The historian revealed certain

Mycenae seems to have imposed its rule on its neighbors in Crete, Cyprus, and Anatolia. Its vigor and violence are expressed in this hunting scene carved on an ivory plaque found in Cyprus (below).

anachronisms and decided that the political and social reality of the Homeric epic was closer to the world of the 8th century BC than of the 2nd millennium. He also stressed the danger and limitations of interpreting an epic text, so given to exaggeration and fantasy. For Finley, the society and tall deeds related by Homer could not be any earlier—at most—than the 10th and 9th centuries BC. Some historians still think, wrongly, that these narratives are linked to the very period of the poet's life, that is, the 8th to 7th century BC.

Archaeological evidence

Other scholars believe that the use of archaic literary expressions, references to places gone or ruined by the

Levels VI and VIIa at Troy yielded numerous Mycenaean objects, attesting to contacts with Greece lasting at least a century. Reconstructed and enlarged following an earthquake, which marks the end of level VI (above), the city was devastated and burned in about 1300 BC. This final destruction, of Troy VIIa, corresponds to the siege by the Greek army as told by Homer.

7th century BC (particularly among the cities that supplied ships for the Trojan expedition), and the presence of elements or behavior that had become obsolete by the time the text was written all indicate borrowings from a very old oral tradition that would include recollections of the Mycenaean period.

Epigraphy and the progress in deciphering Linear B have made a valuable contribution to the debate. The tablets written in Linear B are utilitarian documents (with no claims to literary value) left by palace scribes, particularly at Knossos and Pylos. Although they provide no historic data, they confirm certain Homeric elements concerning political organization and the names of kings or gods, by placing them definitively in the Mycenaean period.

One way of verifying the possible historical value of the text is to look for links between literary allusions

After a siege of ten years, the Greeks managed to take Troy by carrying out a ruse thought up by Odysseus. Greek warriors hid inside a huge horse and left it on the plain of Ilium, and the Trojans brought it inside their walls (above, decoration from a large urn found in Mykonos, dated 670 BC).

and archaeological discoveries. A study by E. S. Sherratt, in fact, has enabled us to distinguish three dynamic phases between the period of the Trojan War and its narration by Homer. During these phases new weapons replaced the old, society was modified by funerary and domestic transformations, and the epic tradition, both oral and, later, written, exalt these changes in the context of a single narration relating the exploits and calamities of the Trojan War.

The first phase corresponds to the period of the old Mycenaean palaces (15th to 14th century BC), the birth of the epic tradition in the Peloponnese, and probably the Trojan War (between Troy VI and VII in Anatolia). Iron is mentioned as having a great mercantile value but is not yet in everyday use. Houses have a stairway leading to the second story and flat roofs. The warriors' arms might include a bronze breastplate of the Dendra type and certainly a helmet made of boar's tusks similar to helmets painted in frescoes and described in poems, as well as a large single spear, a large, pointed Mycenaean sword, and a long shield for hand-to-hand combat.

After the age of Mycenaean palaces, the postpalatial period between 1200 and 800 BC was at first very active, until the fall of Mycenae in about 1100 BC. Linguists have pointed out major revisions in the different regional Greek versions of the archaic narrative. Iron was then in regular use and funerary rites had shifted from burial to cremation. Houses, relatively simple, had a beaten-earth floor and a pitched roof. The soldiers' spears were adapted for combat in rows at a distance; the shield was round, with serrated edges and a handle in the center; the helmet bore horns; the soldier had two small

What Schliemann called "the cup of Nestor" (above), a gold vessel, and a dagger blade decorated with a scene of a lion hunt (below) were both found in Mycenae in Circle A of the shaft graves. They date from the 16th century BC, that is, at least two centuries before the Trojan War. Thanks to modern dating methods, it is now possible to specify the relative positions of the remains and to reconsider the relationships inferred, sometimes too hastily, between archaeological discoveries and the Homeric poems.

spears, like javelins, and a long sword.

The third phase, from 800 to 700 BC, precedes the definitive version of Homer's text. This is the period of the proto-hoplites, with their round shields showing Medusa's head, the "muscled" breastplate of leather or bronze, the crested helmet, long spear, and javelin. These soldiers were building what would be called Magna Graecia.

A comparison between Homer's texts and archaeological evidence reveals that the similarities seem to outweigh the differences. And the Trojan War becomes completely plausible in the context of the Bronze Age. The war brought together the warriors of the Late Bronze Age much as they are found in tombs with their weapons. It speaks not of empires but rather federations of chiefdoms and aristocratic societies that lived in a world of expanded economic horizons. The possibility that the poet included in his setting certain elements of more recent vintage, cannot, however, be ruled out.

Round, serrated shields, horned helmets, and spears make up the arms of the Mycenaean warrior during the final phase of that culture, between 1200 and 800 BC (above, from a vase found on the acropolis at Mycenae). Such arms, along with elements from older cultures, were also described by Homer.

The Trojan War was no doubt selected from a series of similar Bronze Age conflicts that are now totally forgotten. For Europeans it inspired the very concept of a historic event. The sense of history, which arises from an oral tradition and precedes the writing that communicates it, is thus the successor to myth.

From Mycenae to Europe

Mycenae is a brilliant model of Bronze Age society, which fanned out across parts of Europe with the establishment of the first trading posts—from Anatolia to Sicily—prefiguring Magna Graecia, starting in the 14th century BC. This society developed a system of writing and gave rise to the first references to cities and to Greek gods.

This model also demonstrates an undeniable cultural unity, which would assume a historic dimension while taking the name of the far-gazing princess, Europa, cited by Hesiod and Homer, a name applied to the continent by Herodotus in the 5th century BC.

The sheet-bronze breastplate found in Dendra, Greece, and the boar's-tusk helmet, described by Homer, are contemporaneous with the period of the early Mycenaean palaces (15th–14th century BC). These archaeological objects suggest that a historic reality underlay the Homeric legends. Overleaf: a ceramic votive chariot from Crete, 11th century BC, features the bull, venerated on the island of the Minotaur. The myth of the bull that kidnapped Europa arose at the end of the Bronze Age.

DOCUMENTS

"[Hephaistos, son of Zeus and Hera, god of fire]
cast on the fire bronze which is weariless, and tin with it
and valuable gold, and silver, and thereafter set forth
upon its standard the great anvil, and gripped in one hand
the ponderous hammer, while in the other he grasped the pincers."
Homer, *Iliad,* 18:474–77

Ötzi, man of the glacier

On 19 September 1991 a German couple hiking in the Tirol encountered a human mummy in the ice, unaware that they had stumbled upon a man from the Copper Age. Discounting the wild speculations of journalists and even a few specialists, it was archaeologist Konrad Spindler who first made the formal identification. Who was this little man? How had he lived? Studies of his anatomy and equipment, both exceptionally well preserved, revealed many details about the daily life of human beings five thousand years ago.

The man of ice and his times

Immediately after the discovery, many questions arose, which were formulated by archaeologist Henri de Saint-Blanquat.

A body has been discovered…at an altitude of 10,000 feet (3,200 meters) near the Italian-Austrian border, complete with his skin, clothing, and equipment from five thousand years ago and straw in his shoes.…He marshaled the attention of the media, as each journalist struggled to find something a bit different to relate. None succeeded, since this kind of discovery proves to be very short on details. The interesting aspects developed later, when analysis began to yield results. But the fact remains: a body was discovered. That is enough to cause excitement. This is because we have seen so few people from that period. Even in Europe, in fact, we know no one. At first, of course, we recall the famous men of the Danish peat bogs: the man of Borremose, or of Gauballe or Tollünd, the last of these having been found with the rope still around his neck, strangled. This was a case of sacrifice, preceded by a ritual meal, to judge from the remains found in his stomach.…But those corpses are clearly younger than our Bronze Age hunter; they come from the Scandinavian Iron Age, close to the Christian era.

A bit older was the young woman from Egtved, preserved with her skin, hair, tooth enamel, and nails, but without her bones.…She dated from the beginning of the Bronze Age in Scandinavia, about 1400 BC. Nor should we forget the naturally mummified bodies discovered in countries with a drier climate: Egypt, Sudan, Saharan Africa. At Tassili, the site of Ti n'Anakaten had preserved the remains of a child with parts of its skin and hair; this child took us back several thousand years before the Christian era. In the Sudan, the necropolis of the great site of Kerma produced graves of men buried in large skin coverings who were naturally mummified, desiccated. Their date is approximately 3000 BC. This is also the age of the earliest Egyptian mummies. The technique was still far short of perfection (it would reach its peak a few centuries after Ramses), but it benefited from the unusual Egyptian climate. There have been finds of naturally mummified bodies going back to the predynastic era, in the 4th millennium. In terms of exceptional preservation, the record for seniority is held by the men found in a Florida swamp who were more than eight thousand years old. There was also a family of Eskimos discovered a few years ago in Greenland in frozen earth that was only five hundred years old. Thus we see the three environments that favor exceptional preservation: humidity (in an acidic milieu), dryness, and cold (ice or frozen earth). And we also observe that such discoveries are extremely rare.

Thus, it was in the melting ice of the Similaun glacier that this little man (5 feet 4 inches tall, or 1.6 meters) was found. Reports striving for colorful and informative detail said he must have worn a kind of anorak and something resembling boots, made of skin stuffed with straw. For the moment, the objects found with him provided the basis for citing a period, if not for dating. Unfortunately, police officers stripped him entirely before bundling him up in sacks; none of these objects was found exactly in place, and the clothing has suffered a bit....

Nevertheless, the archaeologists were unanimous and the authenticity of the discovery was beyond doubt. The discovery indicated that certain glaciers may contain ancient ice, hemmed in by an obstacle—a potential avenue of research. As a rule, accident victims' corpses that fall into crevasses are expelled by the glacier at its extremity after at most a few decades.

This short man was rather well equipped: a bronze ax, a flint dagger in its sheath, a wooden bow, and fourteen arrows with heads of either stone or bone. What was he doing up there? Was he hunting or was he trying to go from one valley to another? It is in any case the earliest mountain drama we know of. It probably occurred around the beginning of the Bronze Age, according to specialists on the era, judging from this ax whose blade, lightly flanged, in fact recalls the Early Bronze Age....

Bronze is, moreover, the only metal found on this glacier climber. The flint dagger, for its part, recalls earlier periods before the use of metal—but apparently our man could not afford better. As for the arrowheads, they have also proved interesting. In fact, they were attached to the shaft with pitch; a small ball of pitch is seen at the base of each attached head. And, judging from the pitch supply kept in reserve in the sack, the hunters of the time could probably change heads as needed; it was only a matter of melting the pitch and attaching a different head to the arrow.

This man lost up there must have been part of a family, a village, and, of course, a culture. We are best informed about his material culture. North of the Alps, in the heart of Bohemia, the reigning culture was that of Uněrice—a beacon, one of the centers of Bronze Age Europe. The sites associated with Unětice culture have been found from Lower Saxony to Slovakia. Its artisans show a strong tendency to ship their products afar, especially the most valuable, of course, which were riveted daggers....The age of metal weapons had begun. The relative prosperity demonstrated by this civilization must have derived from this bronze, in which it proved something of a pioneer in Europe. The culture was within close range of deposits of copper and especially tin—in the metal-bearing mountains of the Erzgebirge. Soon the bronze smelters began to produce fine flanged axes—lightly flanged at first— of the kind that our mountain man was carrying.

But his dagger was of stone, as in earlier times. Daggers, however, were the most frequently exported product, or the kind that the neighbors of Unětice tried hardest to obtain and to imitate. These Alpine valleys were located about 130 miles (200 kilometers) from the center of Unětice culture, so to some extent they must have felt its influence. But was that center actually the primary influence on them? The corpse, we know, caused some dispute since it was found just barely on the Italian side of the border. Perhaps this is a debate that could be extended to the protohistoric era, since there existed south of the Alps another civilization of the Early Bronze Age, even older than Unětice, and much closer. It covered Lombardy, Veneto, and Trentino, which is an Alpine region. This Polada civilization began in the late 3rd millennium.

Polada, too, produced flanged axes. Thus, it is worth looking closely at the little man's ax, as well as his flint arrowheads, if we hope to determine to which world he belonged—the world of central Europe or the Mediterranean.

Henri de Saint-Blanquat,
"Au temps de l'homme des glaces,"
in *Sciences et Avenir,*
December 1991

An unusual discovery

Six years later, Jean-Pierre Mohen and Christiane Eluère summarized the discovery. It was clear by then, for instance, that Ötzi's ax was made not of bronze but of copper.

The first reaction of the public, the journalists, and many specialists was to refute the age of the mummy because it was in a glacier. Everyone can cite examples of animals or humans ejected at the extremity of a glacier at the same time as moraines. There was no reason, then, why this mummy, Ötzi, should have remained at the summit of the glacier.

The other troubling issue was the remarkable state of preservation of the body and the surrounding archaeological objects, since we would expect a glacier to contain dispersed, ground-up debris. Studies by glaciologists gave support to the arguments explaining the exceptional location of the body and its equipment in a rocky basin at such high altitude at the very base of the glacier, where the snow and ice do not yet exert their force to carry off trees, rocks, or any other element toward the valley.

There was another fundamental question: Why was the mummy still

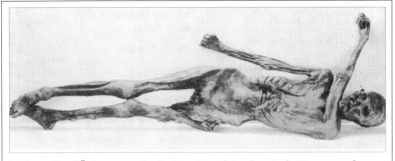

The remains of Ötzi, as preserved today, in an air-conditioned case in the Department of Anatomy of the University of Innsbruck, Austria.

intact as if it had been trapped in the ice shortly after the man's death and had not emerged until the summer of 1991?

The body bears no trace of deterioration that would certainly have been caused by actions of animals or weather if the body had reappeared in the open air in the course of the centuries. Here again, we can assemble a series of exceptional factors to explain that the body had been covered in snow around the month of September, that a warm wind had been able to desiccate the flesh while ice formed and remained at a constant temperature between 32° and 43°F (0 to 6°C)—which is the temperature at which the mummy is preserved henceforth, at a humidity of 99 percent. Ice around the body melted only as the result of two phenomena, the current global warming and the rain of Saharan sands that covered the glacier with a fine sand layer in the spring of 1991, storing up the heat of the day and preventing the formation of new ice at night.

Hardest of all to understand was how a man five thousand years old could reach us still intact, with all his flesh, his organs, his clothing, and his equipment of organic material that normally decomposes after a few years.

Two dating methods were used to pinpoint the man of the glacier's time of death. The first was archaeological. Thus, on the basis of the typology of the copper ax discovered with a handle near the mummy, Konrad Spindler made an initial approximation of 2000 BC, the very beginning of the Bronze Age. The remaining objects, the dagger and flint arrowheads, seem older and could date from at least a thousand years earlier, that is, from the end of the Neolithic or the beginning of the Chalcolithic Ages.

This earlier date now seems clearly indicated by physicochemical methods as the most likely....Results from five different laboratories (at Oxford, Zurich, Uppsala, Cambridge, Massachusetts, and Gif-sur-Yvette, France) are very consistent and give a reasonable span between 3350 and 3100 BC.

J.-P. Mohen and C. Eluère, from "L'Homme des Glaces dans les Alpes il y a 5000 ans," in *Dossiers d'Archéologie*, no. 224 (June 1997)

The marvels of Mt. Bego

The extraordinary site of the Vallée des Merveilles and Mt. Bego has drawn visitors since the 17th century. An Englishman, Clarence Bicknell—who died in 1918 at the foot of the sacred mountain—was the first to devote himself to it, and he spread its fame through his searches and reports. Here, Jean Guilaine considers the depictions of bovines, bronze tools, and figures chipped into the rock and surveyed by the team of Henry de Lumley. Jacques Briard, in turn, examines the anthropomorphic forms.

Myths and labor in the Early Bronze Age

At Mt. Bego near St.-Dalmas-de-Tende in the Alpes-Maritimes, France, at an altitude between 7,000 and 9,000 feet (2,100 to 2,700 meters), populations at the beginning of the ages of metals engraved gray-green schist, sometimes with a pink patina, or hard sandstone with scenes or symbols that are uniquely informative about certain aspects of life during these periods. The total number of these carved depictions is estimated at 100,000—an indication of the remarkable library of rock archives preserved there, despite the harm done by time and above all by humans, including incessant treading, damage to the designs by shameless tourists, careless castings, not to mention attempts to remove engravings. Prehistoric people used the engraving technique of hammering the rock with the help of an instrument with a soft stone or metal point.

The site also contains finely incised engravings from the Roman, medieval, and modern eras. They testify to the perennial traffic of shepherds and their spiritual or material concerns. Once considered older, this linear (or "pre-Merveilles") style has in fact proved to be from more recent, in fact, historic, times. These depictions, moreover, are closely related to those carved on other rocks in southern France, in Hérault or the eastern Pyrenees, for instance.

The prehistoric carvings, the only ones we are concerned with here, can be reduced to a definite number of depictions.

Bovine figures, always schematized, are the most frequent (about 60 percent of the total). Their body is represented

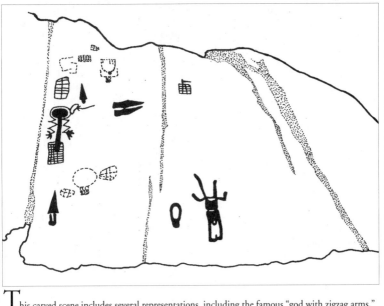

This carved scene includes several representations, including the famous "god with zigzag arms."

by a geometric shape (circle, oval, square, rectangle, trapezoid, or triangle) with horns and, secondarily, other appendages, such as feet, tail, ears. These figures are sometimes seen yoked in twos or fours. They are sometimes depicted towing a plow, depicted by a long wooden rod—the shaft—which extends to a handle on one side and a plowshare on the other. A farmer may be shown driving this rig. A mass of lines sometimes appears behind the cattle, and this can be interpreted as a harrow. These scenes are interesting in that they reveal that the use of the plow was common among agricultural populations of the western Mediterranean in the early 2nd millennium. The stylization of the bovines, with

their horns as the essential feature, suggests a possible cult of the bull and the life forces, widespread since Neolithic times throughout the Mediterranean and given a new impetus by the European Bronze Age.

Bronze implements are also well represented (in about 15 percent of the works). They include weapons or work utensils. Pieces consisting of a triangular blade attached perpendicularly to a long shaft by a series of rivets recall halberds, arms that were typical of the Early Bronze Age. It has been hypothesized, however, that these are scythes because of the appendages at the center and at the end of the shaft. Sickles are depicted as well. Daggers occur frequently, usually with a triangular blade, generally narrow, with handle and sometimes a pommel. The triangular short pieces without a hilt or with a trapezoidal tang are surely the earliest; they have counterparts made of metal in diverse civilizations of the European Copper Age. Elongated blades with a trapezoidal tang or a handle with pommel belong to the beginning of the Bronze Age. Finally, daggers with certain more elaborated elements (oval blades or those with wavy borders) can be placed in the middle of the 2nd millennium. Here we see the importance of the different categories of dagger; they are in fact the best chronological guides for dating the rock art of Mt. Bego.

Of interest as well are the geometric figures, which make up about 20 percent of the themes of the Vallée des Merveilles engravings. They include squares, rectangles, or ovals chipped into the stone in part or completely, whereas others are compartmented, by parallel or crossed lines, within cells that vary in number. How are these shapes to be interpreted? They have been called enclosures or cattle pens; some bovines may be depicted inside them, but we cannot be sure that the enclosure and the animals date from the same period. Other hatched figures filled with chipped points may represent cultivated fields, in which the points would represent grains. Or is this instead an enclosure, a kind of grid chart? This question has puzzled specialists.

Along with these figures closely linked to daily life there are anthropomorphic motifs of a fundamentally different type. Through their scarcity, in fact, these figures acquire a special symbolic or religious force. This is true, for instance, of small men with raised arms, or "orants"; others brandishing halberds; and, finally, those driving plows. But a special place is reserved for certain majestic figures: what is called the head of "Christ," for instance, or the depiction of a "sorcerer," whose face is enclosed by hands near which dagger blades have been placed. Or again, the

Figures of plows drawn by pairs of cattle, typical of the art of Mt. Bego.

"tribal chief" in the praying or orant posture, thumbs in the air, with a knife sunk in his head. Nor should we fail to mention the subject with a circular head and zigzag arms with spread fingers; the head is within a circle in which we see a kind of weapon with handle, either an ax or a club. Another character, with legs and arms flung wide, the torso surrounded with a circle of dots, seems to be performing a kind of dance, possibly an initiation rite. At any rate, this is how popular tradition has perennially interpreted this particular engraving, known for a long time as the "dancing woman" although it is equipped with a well-defined phallus.

What then does Mt. Bego represent? In all probability it is a large, open-air cult area, a land of pilgrimage. Shepherds, farmers, and soldiers of the Alpine and Mediterranean regions must have frequented this extraordinary land and left here, in a symbolic gesture that resulted in engraved archives, irreplaceable testimony of both their daily lives and their spiritual concepts.

Jean Guilaine,
La France d'avant la France:
Du Néolithique à l'âge du fer,
Paris, 1980

The tribal chief

The so-called stela of the tribal chief stands out among the anthropomorphic figures of Mt. Bego.

Anthropomorphs are among the most appealing figures. They are often placed at strategic points: where travelers are obliged to pass, at separations between zones of artwork, or as the final figures at the summit of a mountain. The differences in scale are clear; the smaller ones are simple humans, while the

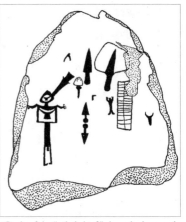

Stela of the "tribal chief," the only decorated unattached block at Mt. Bego.

largest are gods or heroes who dominate the world. They are either isolated or included in veritable "ritual scenes."

The tribal chief is the most fully elaborated representation. It was created on a small erratic block that has been housed in the Tende museum and replaced by an identifying slab stone in order to avoid deterioration. The god has a dagger in his head, a horned sign around his neck as a pendant, and a small phallus. On his left are small anthropomorphs, a razor, daggers, a horned figure, a fragment, and other symbolic signs. The scene can be interpreted as representing the god of thunder reigning over the world of humans, the worlds of war (daggers), agriculture (the rectangle divided into "plots"), and animal husbandry (horned figure).

Jacques Briard,
L'Age du bronze en Europe, économie
et société 2000–800 avant J.-C.,
Paris, 1997

Rock art of the Val Camonica

The Val Camonica, a valley in Lombardy, northern Italy, north of Brescia and northeast of Bergamo, has yielded a treasure of more than 200,000 rock carvings dating from the 6th millennium BC to the Roman and medieval periods. Its residents may be descendants of the Camunians, named for one of the Alpine tribes cited on Emperor Augustus's trophy monument at La Turbie on the Mediterranean coast. These people formed the practice of chipping and painting the rock walls with symbols, objects, and scenes of their daily life. More effectively than any history text, the images they left us illustrate their life, traditions, beliefs, and economic and social activities for a period of more than six thousand years.

The distribution map for rock art in northern Italy indicates the presence of sites dispersed over almost the entire territory. A quantitative analysis, however, shows that 93 percent of the prehistoric figures are located in the Alpine region....

This type of artistic creativity is found here in a peripheral zone, and this characteristic recurs also in other regions. Comparative studies show that in the execution of rock art across the world, preference usually goes to places that were out of the way, difficult to reach (at least until highways existed), and isolated....

Rock art illustrates the history of Alpine settlement, from the penetration of archaic groups of hunters until the arrival of the Romans. It takes us through the gradual introduction of the production of food and the agropastoral colonizations of the Neolithic and Chalcolithic Ages as well as the conceptual, economic, and social vicissitudes that characterize the Bronze and Iron Ages....

Alpine rock art consists basically of engravings, whereas in southern and central Italy it employs either chipping or painting. The difference seems to be basically a question of conservation. Paintings for the most part have not survived. In the Val Camonica the presence of traces of color on certain surfaces and the discovery of coloring materials in excavations conducted under many of the rocks containing art, as well as the discovery of molds and small mortars with remains of coloring agents, show that a good portion of the engravings were intended to be filled in with colors. They were thus meant to look quite different from what we see now. We can conclude from this that

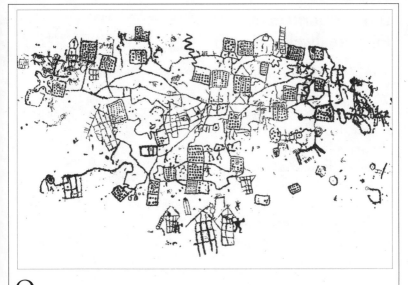

On this stone from Bedolina, the carving seems to depict a map of the environs.

the use of color was widespread, nor can we rule out the possibility that sooner or later, in a cave well protected from weather effects, rock paintings will also be found.

In the Val Camonica the rocks with cup-shaped marks are often found on the periphery of areas with narrative illustrations and along paths that lead to them, as if serving as signals or landmarks on the way to a sacred area. On the other hand, the great rocks with figurative carvings formed immense passages, as at Luina near Boario Terme, Nadro (Ceto), Cimbergo, Paspardo, Cipo di Ponte, and Sellero, which yielded concentrations of more than a hundred narrative areas, each with several thousand figures....The monumental compositions with figures of "solar disks," daggers, axes, halberds, anthropomorphs, and zoomorphs are concentrated especially on the high plateau of Ossimo-Borno for the Val Camonica and on the plateau of Teglio for Valtellina, but some are also found occasionally in other zones.

Emmanuel Anati,
Dossiers d'Archéologie,
no. 224 (June 1997)

Bronze workers of the lake dwellings

The lake villages built on the lakeshores apparently were suddenly submerged in the Late Bronze Age. They left traces that have been particularly well preserved: ruins of wooden houses, tools complete with handles, fabrics and fragments of clothing, cultivated seeds and harvests, pottery and remains of cooked food. These villages occur frequently in the northern Alps, on sites first constructed as early as the Neolithic. They formed veritable economic and defensive centers, small in size but very prosperous; their bronze workers must have been very active.

Specialized craftsmen

The Late Bronze Age seems to mark the apotheosis of the bronze worker's trade, a fact recognized in the term "the high Bronze Age," characterized by the lakeside discoveries. Yet these metals, bronze and tin, were not of local origin, and the earliest copper mines can be found only in the interior Alps, quite far from western Switzerland. Bronze reached this area by trade, in the form of ingots, manufactured objects, or broken fragments intended for recasting.

Between 1100 and 800 BC, each village had at least one blacksmith of its own. To judge from the concentration of clay tuyeres or of hammers, anvils, and foundry casts in some districts, there may already have been a caste or a corporation of bronze workers. They clearly showed an unrivaled mastery of this art of fire. The metal was melted in terra-cotta crucibles and poured into two-piece casts of soft sandstone in a process akin to an assembly line, which turned out identical, high-quality products. No less skillful was their practice of the lost-wax method, which allows any shape to be cast, up to and including the animal forms that decorate the handles of bronze tools.

Bronze in this era became the material of choice for tools and adornment, and metallurgical production was central to all activity. For fishing, metalworkers provided hooks and shuttles for nets, made of bronze, of course. Since the Middle Bronze Age, the farmer's scythe was made of bronze; at times it would have a handle carved to the shape of the hand and fingers to ensure more effective and less tiring work. To harness a horse, the bronze bit soon replaced the bit made of antler, which went out of favor; as for harness straps, they were decorated with plaques and disks of gleaming bronze.

The carpenter and joiner's tools were specialized, including axes with wide or narrow blades, scissors, gouges, and fine-tooth saws. Sewing leathers and fabrics was greatly facilitated by handled awls, bodkins, and needles with eyes. The curved knife was another tool that appeared in the Late Bronze Age. For warfare, long swords became popular, as did ash-handled spears with bronze head and ferrule and arrows with flat, triangular heads.

Not surprisingly, clothing and jewelry also benefited from the smith's innovative techniques. Newly cast bronze has a golden color and an unequaled brilliance after long polishing. Metal combs, razors, and hair tweezers became obligatory for clients straining to meet current standards of beauty, which was heightened as well by bracelets, pins, disk pendants, and belt clasps. People at that time devoted a good part of their efforts to ornament and decoration; the inventive genius of the bronze workers catered to this interest.

The smith was not content with mass production; he exhibited his skill with a masterpiece like the Cortaillod wheel. Its hub and four spokes and the open rim with a V-shaped cross section were cast in just one piece, before receiving an oak tire, secured with eight nails. This wheel must have had a diameter of about 20 inches (50 centimeters). The bronze worker also tried to imitate rare pieces. It was long believed that the

small belt box from Corcelettes (Grandson, Vaud, Switzerland), a sort of small basin richly decorated with spirals, had been imported from northern Europe; its shape, manufacture, and decoration are entirely characteristic of the Danish Bronze Age. Instead, it is believed to be a magnificent imitation by the bronze workers of the Lake of Neuchâtel. The metalsmith, it seems, would try to perfect new techniques and objects; this is demonstrated by a bronze goblet found at Auvernier, which imitates a terra-cotta receptacle decorated with tin sheet.

Toward the end of the period, the lakeside bronze workers became aware of a new metal that was beginning to circulate: iron. At first it could be obtained only in very small quantities. Nevertheless, it began to appear in the form of inlay on bracelets, sword hilts, ferrules of knives. People even went so far as to attach small iron disks to the heads of pins and, the height of luxury, to manufacture a few pins entirely of iron, at Zurich-Alpenquai. This new metal at the time was as rare as gold; it was thus employed as a precious metal, with a color that went well with bronze. A spear from Nidau (Steinberg, Berne) was one of the few to have an iron head, truly functional, on which a bronze socket was cast for securing the shaft.

There can be no doubt that bronze work by the lakeside was an elaborate craft, expanding rapidly, capable of responding quickly to the demands of a sizable clientele in a society that already gave signs of early urban organization.

Pierre Pétrequin,
Gens de l'eau, gens de la terre,
Paris, 1984

Literature of the Bronze Age

Toward the end of the Bronze Age, written accounts of older traditional folkloric materials began to appear. It is believed that Homer wrote the Iliad *based on older oral stories in the 8th century* BC; *the earliest sections of the Old Testament were collected and put in narrative form beginning in the 10th century* BC. *In both of these works, metals, especially bronze, are associated with warfare. In the Old Testament, the development of technology can be seen as a retreat from virtue. Tubalcain, the first blacksmith, is a descendant of Cain and the son of Zillah, which means shade. In* Works and Days, *Hesiod, writing in 7th-century* BC *Greece, created as categories the earlier ages of metals, from gold to bronze, the last "hard of heart like adamant, fearful men" who "loved the lamentable works of Ares and deeds of violence."*

David and Goliath

As the armies of the Philistines and the men of Israel under Saul prepared for battle, the giant Goliath challenges a single man to fight him. The young shepherd David volunteers to go against him.

And there went out a champion out of the camp of the Philistines, named Goliath, of Gath, whose height was six cubits and a span.

And he had a helmet of brass upon his head, and he was armed with a coat of mail; and the weight of the coat was five thousand shekels of brass.

And he had greaves of brass upon his legs, and a target of brass between his shoulders.

And the staff of his spear was like a weaver's beam; and his spear's head weighed six hundred shekels of iron....

And he stood and cried unto the armies of Israel, and said unto them, Why are ye come out to set your battle in array? Am I not a Philistine, and ye servants to Saul? Choose you a man for you, and let him come down to me.

If he be able to fight with me, and to kill me, then will we be your servants: but if I prevail against him, and kill him, then shall ye be our servants, and serve us....

And [David] took his staff in his hand, and chose him five smooth stones out of the brook, and put them in a shepherd's bag which he had, even in a scrip; and his sling was in his hand: and he drew near to the Philistine....

And when the Philistine looked about, and saw David, he disdained him: for he was but a youth, and ruddy, and of a fair countenance.... And the Philistine cursed David by his gods....

Then said David to the Philistine, Thou comest to me with a sword, and with a spear, and with a shield: but I come to thee in the name of the Lord of hosts, the God of the armies of Israel, whom thou hast defied.

This day will the Lord deliver thee into mine hand; and I will smite thee, and take thine head from thee....

And all this assembly shall know that the Lord saveth not with sword and spear: for the battle is the Lord's, and he will give you unto our hands.

And it came to pass, when the Philistine arose, and came and drew nigh to meet David, that David hasted, and ran toward the army to meet the Philistine.

And David put his hand in his bag, and took thence a stone, and slang it, and smote the Philistine in his forehead, that the stone sunk into his forehead; and he fell upon his face to the earth.

1 Samuel 17:4–50, King James Version

Paris and Menelaus

After the Greeks (the Achaians) have made war on Troy for nine years, Paris (also known as Alexandros), whose abduction of Helen touched off the strife, agrees to fight Menelaus, Helen's husband, one-on-one to resolve the conflict.

First [Alexandros] placed along his legs
the fair greaves linked with
silver fastenings to hold the greaves at
the ankles.
Afterwards he girt on about his chest
the corselet
of Lykaon his brother since this fitted
him also.
Across his shoulders he slung the sword
with the nails of silver,
a bronze sword, and above it the great
shield, huge and heavy....
He took up a strong-shafted spear that
fitted his hand's grip.
In the same way warlike Menelaos put
on his armour.

Now when these two were armed on
either side of the battle,
they strode into the space between the
Achaians and Trojans,
looking terror at each other; and
amazement seized the beholders,
Trojans, breakers of horses, and strong-
greaved Achaians.
They took their stand in the measured
space not far from each other
raging each at the other man and
shaking their spearshafts.
First of the two Alexandros let go his
spear far-shadowing
and struck the shield of Atreus' son on
its perfect circle
nor did the bronze point break its way
through, but the spearhead bent back
in the strong shield. And after him
Atreus' son, Menelaos
was ready to let go the bronze spear,
with a prayer to Zeus father:
"Zeus, lord, grant me to punish the
man who first did me injury,
brilliant Alexandros, and beat him
down under my hands' strength
that any one of the men to come may
shudder to think of
doing evil to a kindly host, who has
given him friendship."
So he spoke, and balanced the spear
far-shadowed, and threw it
and struck the shield of Priam's son on
its perfect circle.
All the way through the glittering shield
went the heavy spearhead
and smashed its way through the
intricately worked corselet;
straight ahead by the flank the
spearhead shore through his tunic,
yet he bent away to one side and
avoided the dark death.

Homer, *Iliad*, 3:330–60,
trans. Richmond Lattimore,
Chicago, 1951

The Bronze Age in the world

The use of copper and bronze corresponds all over the world to a particular new technology, economic system, and social organization. While each region of each continent is unique in its way, it is also true that metallurgy and goldworking tend to be associated, as in Europe, with the production of emblems of a strong, heroic authority.

Metalworking in pharaonic Egypt

Egypt experienced a Copper Age and a Bronze Age that coincided with the peak of the pharaonic system.

It is necessary to understand that Egyptian artisans working in metal in the age of the pharaohs were brought together in workshops affiliated with the rulers and the great temples, and that during periods of prosperity they turned out hundreds of tons of material. The great metallurgical and goldsmithing centers were at Thebes in the domain of the great temple of Amen and at Memphis with the temples of the gods Ptah and Sokar, protectors of bronze workers. The Nile Delta region, which received a large share of the copper and tin ingots from the Near East, naturally became active in metallurgy. Ruins of foundries have been excavated at Avaris-Tell Dabah, and the arms factories of the Ramses have just been discovered at Pi-Ramses-Qantir.

Thus, the archaeological sources complement the written sources and the

This relief from the tomb of Rekhmire shows workers melting bronze in a crucible, then pouring it into molds.

iconography of a number of paintings and bas-reliefs. The paintings concern metal in general, that is, cuprous metals and precious metals. When the name of the metal is specified, like electrum in the tomb of Mereruka, we observe that the techniques of melting and casting are the same as those developed for copper. Specific shaping techniques are recognized for goldsmithing.

Reduction furnaces for copper ore have been discovered near the mines. Three of them were excavated at Bouhen, dating from the Old Kingdom (2700–2200 BC); these are stone cylinders open at the top with openings at the base, perhaps for natural drainage, since no pipes have been found, although the presence of ore and slag indicates that high temperatures were reached to perform the reduction. The furnaces at Timna in the Sinai date from the New Kingdom (1555–1030 BC); they include at their base a system of nozzles through which air could be blown in to raise the temperature as high as 660°F (350°C).

Furnaces for smelting depicted in paintings and bas-reliefs are of two types, depending on the period:

During the Old Kingdom they are high and narrowing at the top; the clearest depiction is the one on the tomb of Mereruka.

During the New Kingdom, ovens are wider and lower. The painting on the tomb of Rekhmire [at left] is the most famous.

After the casting
Numerous tools were necessary for a series of operations following casting; these include hammers, scissors, chisels, bodkins, and polishing stones. Hammering was performed by small masses of polished stone, discoid or hemispherical in shape, held even with the hand. The anvil or tas was a simple block of stone, hard chalk, or basalt. In the New Empire the anvil was elevated on a wooden block. We do not know what motions the artisans performed or, in particular, how they manipulated the metal during heating or hammering. They must have used some tool other than pincers, of which no traces have been found. The shaping of vessels and cauldrons required various techniques. For open forms, sheet metal was stamped inside a hollow indentation in a kind of matrix anvil; in this way the interior of a plate or bowl was hammered. For closed forms a long ramrod was used; its rounded end went into the vase and served as a support for hammering the belly on the outside. The first of these techniques corresponds to stamping, the second to reducing.

Introduction of bronze to sub-Saharan Africa

According to Herodotus, metallurgical skills introduced by the Phoenicians to Carthage in the 9th century BC were spread as far as Mauritania and along the Niger valley. The discovery of tin in the Nok valley in Nigeria gave rise to a brilliant civilization that flowered from the early 1st millennium BC. Its production prefigured the bronzes made with tin and lead, the royal products from Igbo Ukuvu starting in the 9th century AD, those from Ife from the 11th century, and those from Benin from the 12th century. Bronze metallurgy linked to the spread of iron is also typical of the kingdom of Great Zimbabwe in East Africa, marked by a remote Egyptian and Sudanese heritage.

From the Copper to the Bronze Age in the Near and Middle East

Mesopotamia has no ore. However, it was familiar with metal since the 5th millennium BC by way of relations with Persia (Iran) and the copper mines of the Anarak region.

After three or four millennia of copper metallurgy, alloys appeared starting in the 4th millennium. The treasure of the cave of Nahal Mishmar in Israel consists of 416 cult items, including 400 prestige pieces made from particular alloys of arsenic and antimony. The addition of tin to form classic bronze did not show up until later.

About 2600 BC bronze was mentioned in Mesopotamia in the archaic texts of Ur and Fara, which make a distinction between *urudu,* copper, and *zabar,* bronze. A text from Lagash even gives the proportion of six parts of copper for one part of tin, or 12 percent tin. This alloy was considered a precious metal at the time, and it was no accident if its presence was noted alongside that of gold in royal contexts at Ur and Susa. Tin at the time came primarily from the east, from Uzbekistan or Afghanistan, and served the workshops of Mesopotamia and Susiana, whereas metallurgy in central Asia favored more traditional alloys, such as copper-arsenic and copper-lead. On the other hand, copper no longer originated in Iran but instead in the land of Oman. Recent analyses by the research laboratory of the Museums of France performed on coppers from Susa, characterized by trace elements like cobalt, nickel, and iron, suggest a connection between these metallic objects and certain ores extracted in a region bordering the Gulf of Oman, 900 miles (1,300 kilometers) from Susa. Copper was sent in the form of ingots, which often had to be refined; texts from Ur III show that this operation consisted in melting the copper in a crucible while adding a flux, antimony, arsenic, and even tin, oil, or salt to collect the impurities and reduce oxidation. Copper was a precious raw material that was used, like other metals, as a medium of exchange often mentioned in contracts. The Lagash tablets clearly indicate that such transactions were carried out by merchants for the prince and his wife.

At the end of the 3rd millennium BC, relations between countries could extend over long distances; thus, at Susa in Elam are proofs of contacts with Bactria, Baluchistan, the Indus, the Syrian coast, and Cappadocia. Metallurgy benefited from these exchanges, and the use of tin in particular became more common. Bronze at that time served to mold weapons and adzes and to assemble elements of chariots. New techniques included the production of gouges with

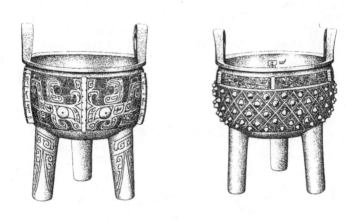

In China bronze work dates back to the end of the 3rd millennium, benefiting from important ore deposits. Metallurgical activity was official. Here, ritual vases of the Shang dynasty (2nd millennium BC).

octagonal cross section and the casting of a hilt on the tang of a dagger. Luristan was then a leader in manufacturing cast bronzes using the lost-wax method, producing axes engraved with narrative scenes like those found in Bactria.

Early bronze in India and the Far East

While the valley of the Indus and its urban civilization at Harappa seemed to maintain a long tradition of copper metallurgy, some technical innovations arose in connection with metallic statuettes produced by the lost-wax method and small gold jewelry that appeared starting in the 5th millennium BC. Bronze as such, using tin, seems unknown until about the mid-2nd millennium, when bronze objects were included among funerary offerings placed inside tumuli in central India.

The originality of ancient bronze metallurgy in China and the Far East in general justifies the idea of an autonomous development. Bronze, derived from ore containing copper and tin, appeared early in China, starting in the late 3rd millennium, and also very quickly, just a few centuries after the appearance of the first copper products. In some cases, the alloy seems to have been the first metal used.

The exploited copper ores were oxides and carbonates; reduction of sulfurs was apparently not yet mastered. Techniques in currency all involved casting; the resulting Chinese bronzes, such as ritual vases of the Erlitu civilization (2nd millennium), were not hammered and thus proved less durable. Casting techniques later predominated in the making of iron objects as well. The technique of forging was not fully developed until the second half of the 1st millennium BC.

Other metals, such as gold and silver, saw little use in ancient times. Though a small number of gold objects from the end of the 3rd millennium BC are known, nothing in silver appears until the 6th century BC.

Japan also evolved a tradition of bronze casting, as seen in the bells of the Yayoi civilization at the end of the 1st millennium BC.

American Bronze Age, late and concentrated

Goldsmithing in the Americas, especially in the Andes, exploited alloys and invented techniques for precious metals around the second half of the 1st millennium BC. Copper was used for tools; the alloy of copper and tin, classic bronze, does not appear until the 15th century AD, introduced by the Incas.

In the Mochica culture, from 200 BC, the alloy of copper and silver, developed along with the exploitation of pure copper, presented two metallurgical advantages: its hardness and its ability to be enriched with silver on the surface when hammered and reheated. This alloy of 10 percent or more silver was most commonly employed in sheet-metal form to make adornments and figures. In later periods, Chimu (AD 1000 to 1476) and Chincha, it was used to make vases. It could be composed of up to 74 percent silver, 23 percent copper, and 3 percent gold.

Copper containing silver also was present even in the central Andes. The latter made up 6 to 18 percent of this ore by weight, producing an alloy of 20 percent silver and 80 percent copper.

During the same Mochica era, another alloy, called *tumbaga*—made of copper and gold—was also common. It was often compounded with silver. An ingot from the Moche valley, for example, was composed of 60 percent copper, 30 percent gold, and 10 percent silver. This kind of alloy was worked in sheet form or was molded in the lost-wax method. Its golden color made it particularly desirable, and there were several ways of enriching the surface with gold. For a copper-gold alloy, one could heat the metal sufficiently to produce copper oxides, which could then be removed by hammering; a copper-gold-silver alloy (silver being the most difficult to remove) had to be worked with an organic acid or mineral. This technique…was used during the Chimu era. Metallurgists could produce golden surfaces on objects with only 12 percent gold by weight. This method was also in practiced in Mexico when the Spanish arrived in Central America at the beginning of the 16th century.

This ceremonial knife from Peru combining gold and silver dates to about 1300 BC.

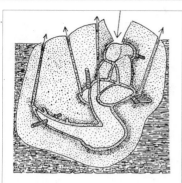

These technologies had an impact on the organization of society; arsenical copper was particular to the rural population, while bronze made with tin became the metal of the Inca civilization.

The lost-wax casting method: the wax model melts and leaves its imprint in the mold when the metal is poured in.

An important technological change seems to have developed during the Chimu epoch in northern Peru, when the alloy of copper and arsenic became the predominant metal. This copper alloy was the metal of choice in the production of tools and instruments and became important to agriculture and the economy in general. It was obtained from a mixture of oxidized and carbonated copper and sulfide ores containing arsenic which had to be roasted before being poured into the reduction furnace. As minerals found along the coast ceased to be suitable, sulfur had to be imported from the high plateaus, thus increasing the traffic between these two regions.

Copper with arsenic was replaced during the age of the Incas (1476–1534) by bronze made with tin. The choice seems to have been a deliberate one, which was then imposed, like the Quechua language, on the entire Andean region. The two are considered the essential elements of unity, standardization, and control on the economic, political, and cultural levels.

Thus, bronze made with tin competed against arsenical bronze for reasons that were more ideological than technological. From a technological point of view, a difference between the two bronze alloys can be discerned. From AD 1000, the dominance of the bronze alloy with tin spread in the southern Andes. Authorities agree that cassiterite, which was found in abundance in Bolivia (Lake Titicaca) and northern Argentina, was mined solely for the production of this alloy. Tin oxide, which had been extracted from silt deposits and underground veins, was reduced by being mixed directly with the oxides or carbonates of copper. Or, more probably, it was first reduced and then put in the crucible. Thus, the metallurgy of bronze made with tin is less complex than that with arsenic, which favored the ascendance of the Incas.

Jean-Pierre Mohen,
*Métallurgie préhistorique:
Introduction à la paléométallurgie,*
Paris, 1990

Chronology

Date (BC)	Egypt	Aegean Continental Greece	Crete	Cyclades	Central Europe
500	Late Period	Classical Age			
600		Archaic Age			*Final Hallstatt*
700		*Homer*	Geometric Period		Early Iron Age
800	Third Intermediate Period				
900		Proto-Geometric Period			Final Bronze Age
1000		Sub-Mycenaean / Late Helladic	Sub-Minoan		
1100		*Fall of Mycenae*			Late Bronze Age
1200	New Kingdom / *Ramses III*		Late Minoan	Late Cycladic	
1300		*Trojan War*			
1400	*Ramses II* / *Amenhotep IV*				Middle Bronze Age
1500	Second Intermediate Period				
1600					
1700			Middle Minoan	Middle Cycladic	*Unětice culture*
1800	Middle Kingdom	Middle Helladic			Early Bronze Age
1900	First Intermediate Period				
2000					
2100					
2200			Early Minoan		*Bell Beaker culture*
2300				Early Cycladic	
2400					
2500	Old Kingdom	Early Helladic			
2600					*Corded Ware culture*
2700					
2800					*Horgen/Wartberg culture*
2900	Predynastic Period				
3000					Late Neolithic/Chalcolithic

Date (BC)	Northern Europe	Iberian Peninsula	British Isles	France	Italy
500	Pre-Roman Iron Age				
600			Iron Age	Early Iron Age	Orientalizing Period
700		*Tartessos*			*Founding of Rome*
800	Late Bronze Age	Orientalizing Period			*Villanova*
900					
1000		Late Bronze Age	*Deverel-Rimbury groups*	Late Bronze Age	*Proto-Villanova* Final Bronze Age
1100	Middle Bronze Age				
1200					Late Bronze Age
1300		Middle Bronze Age		*Atlantic culture Bignan*	
1400					
1500				Middle Bronze Age	
1600				*Tréboul*	Middle Bronze Age
1700	Early Bronze Age				
1800			*Wessex culture*		
1900	*Battle-axes* Late Neolithic	*El Argar*		*Armorican tumulus*	
2000				Early Bronze Age	
2100			Chalcolithic		Early Bronze Age
2200					
2300					
2400	*Megaliths*	Chalcolithic			
2500				Chalcolithic	
2600	Middle Neolithic *Culture of individual tombs*				
2700					
2800					Chalcolithic
2900	*Culture of goblets with twisted-cord handles*				
3000		*Megaliths* Late Neolithic	*Megaliths* Late Neolithic	*Megaliths* Late Neolithic	Late Neolithic

Further Reading

Briard, J., *L'Age du bronze en Europe (2000–800 av. J.-C.)*, 1985

Chadwick, J., *Reading the Past: Linear B and Related Scripts*, 1987

Christopoulos, G. A., and Bastias, J. C., *Prehistory and Protohistory: History of the Hellenic World*, 1970

Coles, J. M., and Harding, A., *The Bronze Age in Europe*, 1979

Dani, A. H., and Mohen, J.-P., *History of Humanity*, vol. 2, *From the Third Millennium to the Seventh Century BC*, 1996

Demakopoulou, K., et al., *Gods and Heroes of the European Bronze Age*, 1999

Eluère, C., *The Celts: Conquerors of Ancient Europe*, Discoveries, 1993

Emlyn-Jones, C., Hardwick, L., and Purkis, J., *Homer: Readings and Images*, 1992

Europe au temps d'Ulysse: Dieux et héros de l'âge du bronze, exh. cat., National-museum, Copenhagen et al., 1999

Guilaine, J., *La France d'avant la France: Du Néolithique à l'âge du fer*, 1980

Harding, A. F., *The Mycenaeans and Europe*, 1984

Homer, *The Iliad of Homer*, trans. Richmond Lattimore, 1951

——, *The Odyssey*, trans. Robert Fitzgerald, 1961

Jensen, J., *The Prehistory of Denmark*, 1995

Müller-Karpe, H., *Handbuch der Vorgeschichte*, vol. 4, *Bronzezeit*, 1980

Renfrew, C., *The Emergence of Civilization: The Cyclades and the Aegean in the Third Millennium BC*, 1972

Spindler, Konrad, *The Man in the Ice*, trans. E. Osers, 1994.

List of Illustrations

Index

Acknowledgments

The authors and publisher express special thanks to Jacques Briard, Katia Demakopoulou, Annie Fortune, Jean Guilaine, Jorgen Jensen, Albrecht Jöckenhövel, Catherine Louboutin, Pascale Martinat, Patrick Périn, as well as Suzanne Bosman, Chantal Dulos at the Musée des Antiquités Nationales in St.-Germain-en-Laye, France, and the *Dossiers d'Archéologie*.

Photograph Credits

AKG, Paris front cover, 4, 16, 30b–31b, 31a, 62b, 77. Archives Gallimard 40. Archives Gallimard Jeunesse 13, 20a, 21b, 27. Artephot-Bapier 124a. Artephot-Nimatallah 11, 86b, 128. Artephot-Oronoz 38a. J. Briard 56a, 92l, 119a. The Bridgeman Art Library, Paris 12, 41b, 47b, 104. British Library 20b–21b. British Museum 120b–121b. G. Dagli Orti, Paris front cover above, 5, 8–9, 25a, 25c, 38b, 46–47, 50–51, 52a, 52b, 53, 65a, 67, 69, 70–71, 72–73, 74b, 82a–83a, 83b, 84, 86a, 87, 88a–89a, 89b, 90, 91, 93a, 94l, 95r, 96a, 96b–97b, 98–99, 100b–101b, 102a, 103, 105, 106c–107c, 107a, 108, 120b–121b, 124b–125b, 125a, 126, 127. D. R. 32, 55a, 64, 76b, 99a, 106a, 115b, 135, 136, 139. Edigraphie 29, 58–59, 75a, 120. G. Gester/Rapho 68. P. Hanny/Gamma 34–35. Laboratoires des Musées de France 22l, 23a, 23b, 26, 42a, 42b, 116a–117a. Editions Ch. Beck, H. Müller-Karpe 1, 2, 3, 4, 5, 6, 7, 8, 9, 39, 54, 60, 62, 65, 115a, 144, 146, 147. Editions Millet/F. Brosse 48–49. Erich Lessing/Magnum front cover below, 1, 3, 25b, 30a, 61a, 76a, 82b, 95b, 101a, 121a. H. Maurer 133. Médialp 33b. Musée des Antiquités Nationales, St.-Germain-en-Laye 41a. Musée Cantonal d'Archéologie, Neuchâtel, M. Egloff 110, 112–13. National Museum of Athens 46b, 109. The National Museum of Denmark, Copenhagen 17b, 18l, 18a–19a, 19b, 78, 79a, 80, 81, 92r. Photothèque des Musées de la Ville de Paris 17a. NMN front cover, spine, back cover, 2, 6, 7, 14b–15b, 28b, 55b, 57, 60b–61b, 63, 85, 93b, 100l, 111, 116l, 117r, 118a, 118b–119b, 130. Roger-Viollet 22b, 43. Römisch-Germanisches Zentral-museum, Mainz/Christian Beeck 36–37. Royal Pavilion and Library, London 14a. Vaisse/Hoa Qui 66.

Text Credits

The Íliad of Homer, translated by Richmond Lattimore © copyright 1951 by The University of Chicago. All rights reserved. Excerpt from "Book Seventeen: The Beggar at the Manor" from THE ODYSSEY OF HOMER translated by Robert Fitzgerald. Copyright © 1961, 1963 by Robert Fitzgerald. Copyright renewed 1989 by Benedict R.C. Fitzgerald, on behalf of the Fitzgerald children. Reprinted by permission of Farrar, Straus and Giroux, LLC

Jean-Pierre Mohen, director of the research laboratory of the French National Museums since 1992, has curated numerous exhibitions at the Grand Palais in Paris (*Scythian Gold*, 1975; *Treasures of the Celtic Princes*, 1987; *The Vikings*, 1992) and was the commissioner for the French Year of Archaeology in 1989–90. His published works include *The World of the Megaliths* (1990), *La Métallurgie préhistorique* (1990), and *Megaliths: Stones of Memory* (New Horizons, 1998). From 1987 to 1992, Mohen was director of the Musée des Antiquités Nationale, St.-Germain-en-Laye, France.

Christiane Eluère, chief curator of the French National Museums, was responsible for the Bronze Age collection of the Musée des Antiquités Nationale, St.-Germain-en-Laye, and is attached to the research laboratory of the French National Museums. Among other exhibitions, she organized *Europe in the Time of Ulysses*, conceived in conjunction with Jean-Pierre Mohen and presented from 1998 to 2000 in Copenhagen, Bonn, Paris, and Athens. Her publications include *L'Or des Celtes* (1987), *Secrets de l'or antique* (1990), and *The Celts: Conquerors of Ancient Europe* (New Horizons, 1993).

Translated from the French by David and Dorie Baker

First published in the United Kingdom in 2000 by Thames & Hudson Ltd, 181A High Holborn, London WC1V 7QX

English translation © 2000 Harry N. Abrams, Inc., New York

© 1999 Gallimard

British Library Cataloguing-in-Publication Data

A catalogue record for this book is available from the British Library

ISBN 0–500–30101–8

Printed and bound in Italy by Editoriale Lloyd, Trieste